NATURALLY
NOURISHED

Clarkson Potter/Publishers
New York

NATURALLY
healthy, delicious meals made
with everyday ingredients

NOURISHED

 SARAH BRITTON

Library of Congress Cataloging-in-Publication Data
Names: Britton, Sarah, author.
Title: Naturally nourished / Sarah Britton.
Description: First edition. | New York : Clarkson Potter/Publishers, [2017] | Includes bibliographical references and index.
Identifiers: LCCN 2016008218 (print) | LCCN 2016019803 (ebook) | ISBN 9780804185400 (hardcover) | ISBN 9780804185417 (eBook) | ISBN 9780804185417 (ebook)
Subjects: LCSH: Vegetarian cooking. | Cooking (Natural foods) | Nutrition. | LCGFT: Cookbooks.
Classification: LCC TX837 .B816 2017 (print) | LCC TX837 (ebook) | DDC 641.5/636—dc23

LC record available at https://lccn.loc gov/2016008218

ISBN 978-0-8041-8540-0
eBook ISBN 978-0-8041-8541-7

Printed in China
Book and cover design by La Tricia Watford
Front cover and interior photography by Sarah Britton

10 9 8 7 6 5 4 3 2 1

First Edition

To Mikkel and Finn, for the everlasting exchange of nourishment

CONTENTS

INTRODUCTION

___

It was just a head of cabbage sitting on my cutting board—humble, unassuming, and quiet, not sexy like a strawberry. Not proud and convincing like broccoli, nor dignified or elegant like a carrot. Yet it was inexpensive, a staunch staple in my supermarket, and I wanted to make it shine. Play with it. Do *something* interesting with that lowly head or I would lose all faith that simple, common vegetables could be transformed to be something truly special. That I don't have to go to the farmers' market to create an inspired meal. And that I wouldn't have to slave over the stove to get dinner on the table.

I sliced the cabbage head into quarters, heated some vegetable broth, simmered the wedges, then set them in a searing-hot pan to char. That modest brassica was completely transformed into something so delicious that I could hardly contain my excitement. It was smoky and savory and rich. I whipped together a sauce with toasted walnuts and garlic, added some chopped apple and parsley, and quite suddenly I had created a meal with intense and complex flavors from such simple ingredients that it felt like the culinary triumph of my life.

After receiving yet another letter from a student asking me how she can eat healthy on her limited food budget and crazy work schedule, I considered the cabbage dish I had made the night before and realized *that* was the answer. Yes, I get jazzed about exotic ingredients, but really, the bulk of my diet consists of vegetables, fruit, legumes, and grains that don't need a lot of doctoring up. In fact, most of my favorite ingredients are found at my neighborhood grocery store. Those letters inspired me to create recipes that everybody can cook from, on almost any budget, any day of the week. Those letters inspired me to write this book.

We all know the importance of eating balanced, nourishing foods, but for many of us, the challenge of creating a healthy dinner can feel overwhelming when we think we have to make special trips to upscale grocers or health food stores for expensive ingredients, buy produce we can't use up, and cook with techniques we may not be familiar with—on top of our day-to-day responsibilities. In fact, hyping up dinner to be a fancy affair can have the opposite intended effect: we can set ourselves up for failure. I want to help you overcome these challenges by giving you the building blocks for creating easy, delicious meals with basic pantry ingredients and affordable produce, using simple-to-master cooking skills. With time I hope you will gain enough confidence to riff on these recipes and make your own meals—and get excited about being creative in the kitchen.

This collection of recipes celebrates all the simple and good ingredients that you probably have in your fridge or that you can get right around the corner. If you are lucky enough to live near a nice supermarket, health food store, or farmers' market, you're sure to find even more organic, local produce and inspiration there.

What writing this book has taught me is that healthy, delicious food doesn't have to be expensive or complicated. I have pushed, learned, and high-fived myself more times during its creation than ever before, because up against the challenge, I have proved that we can eat well, even on a budget, even on a Tuesday.

INSPIRED WEEKNIGHT RECIPES

The book is laid out in five chapters loosely following the seasons—each chapter starting with spring and flowing through the year—but you can make these recipes all year round with produce available to you.

The first two chapters feature Satisfying Soups and Sumptuous Salads. Although the recipes in these chapters can be served as side dishes, all of them are filling enough to be the centerpiece of a busy weeknight meal.

You'll notice that most recipes include a "Rollover" note. This shows you how one recipe rolls into another with leftover elements and will give you ideas on how to cook a bit more of one element (for example, chickpeas) to get a head start on another recipe in the book. This makes tomorrow's meal a whole lot easier: when using rollovers, you can easily plan your week of meals and groceries and save a lot of time. Rollovers are explained in more detail on page 11.

The Nourishing Mains chapter is full of unique and surprising ideas on how to transform grocery store basics into exciting main dishes. Although these recipes aren't complicated, they have a few more ingredients than the recipes in the other chapters. This is where the "Rollover" boxes become especially handy, because they will prompt you to cook enough of one ingredient to make two meals.

The next chapter is Simple Sides and Small Plates. These dishes contain few ingredients and come together quickly, but will surprise you with their big, bold flavors. Each recipe can easily be turned into a main dish simply by using the ideas in the "Sides Me Up!" box. If you're just starting out with healthy cooking, this is in fact a great chapter to begin with, as the recipes are fast and easy. The Sides and Small Plates are meant to accompany main dishes, or you can make several of them together to create a family-style spread.

Savory and Sweet Snacks round out the book with little nibbles perfect for the four-o'clock munchies. Dips, spreads, crackers, and the like also make fantastic appetizers, and combining them creates an impressive spread for special occasions. The healthy, sweet snacks are perfect for all-day enjoyment from breakfast to dessert, and many of them are portable, so they make luxurious lunchbox stuffers!

Each chapter opens with "3 Ways": a recipe with a simple base that you can easily change up—everything from kale salad to chocolate brownie bites. Have fun with this one, and once you get the momentum going, create "3 Ways" of your very own. Also, the recipes are appropriately labeled with symbols so you can easily plan your meals: "V" for vegan, "GF" for gluten-free, "R" for raw, and "GrF" for grain-free.

SIMPLIFY LIFE IN THE KITCHEN

———

There are so many wonderful ways to save time in the kitchen, and even if you love to cook as much as I do, I'm sure you also love spending your precious hours doing other things as well.

BUILDING BLOCKS FOR EVERY MEAL

I approach cooking by looking at ingredients as building blocks. First, I create the foundation of the meal, which can be anything from grains to legumes, a vegetable, or leafy greens. Once I have this in place, I add other elements to make the dish interesting, such as roasted veggies, avocado, hummus, or even a soft-boiled egg. I can actually stop at this point if I don't have any more time, and I end up with a simple yet delicious little meal. If I do have more time, however, I'll make it special by adding some sprouts, salsa, and/or goat cheese, followed by a sauce or dressing. If I'm feeling really ambitious, I'll toast up some seeds, mince some herbs, or chop fresh chiles to give the meal some flair.

Building blocks allow you to compose a dish based on an understanding of what it takes to make a delicious meal, instead of getting hung up on specific ingredients. Using this approach also enables you to identify the roles of the various ingredients in a specific dish so you can easily adjust and customize them depending on what you already have in your fridge or pantry, what season it is, dietary preferences, and tastes. You can even change up old favorite recipes just by swapping out building blocks to create something totally new. Cooking becomes much more convenient, creative, free, and fun!

An example of this approach is one dish that I eat very often for dinner: salads. Simply build your meal:

BUILD A FOUNDATION	MAKE IT INTERESTING	ADD SOMETHING SPECIAL	SAUCE IT UP (optional)	GIVE IT SOME FLAIR (optional)
quinoa	carrots	green lentils	Minty Tahini Dressing (page 63)	Dukkah (page 26)
brown rice	sweet potato	chickpeas	Romesco Sauce (page 195)	cilantro
massaged kale	black lentils	soft-boiled egg	Chermoula (page 148)	crushed red pepper flakes
whole-grain noodles or pasta	broccoli	mung bean sprouts (see Basic Sprouts, page 23)	Almond Butter Sauce (page 135)	Sesame Salt (page 157)
couscous	avocado	black beans	Radish Cilantro Salsa (page 108)	toasted pumpkin seeds
whole roasted sweet potato	black beans	Spicy Lime Slaw (page 99)	Spicy Tahini Ginger Sauce (page 104)	toasted pecans
polenta	roasted beets	goat cheese	Lemon-Mint Date Sauce (page 57)	Ginger-Pickled Carrots (page 87)
whole-grain bread	Basic Hummus (page 187) or other bean spread	Lentil Sprouts (see Basic Sprouts, page 23)	Arugula Pesto (page 141)	chopped olives

ROLLOVERS (COOKING MORE ON PURPOSE)

I've come up with a way to eat well every day without spending much time cooking at all, using what I call *rollovers*. A rollover is an intentional leftover that rolls right on into the next day, or even weeks.

For example, on Monday I cook quinoa for a big quinoa salad (see page 91), but I'll make double so that I have a rollover for Tuesday. Tuesday I'll cook double the lentils that I need for a quinoa and lentil dish, and I'll use the extra lentils for a Wednesday rollover. Wednesday I'll cook a big pot of brown rice to mix with the lentils, and so on.

Rollovers not only work with basic staples, but also with things like roasted vegetables, pie dough, quick pickles, nut butter, seed cheese, toppings, dressing, and sauces. You will in fact see examples of this in almost every recipe in the book. If you can spend more of your kitchen time "assembling" rather than standing over a hot stove, cooking becomes a lot more fun and playful. Yes, there will be investment days when you'll make a big batch of granola bars, salad dressing, and

brown rice, but then you'll have building blocks for many meals. You'll see your fridge and pantry filling up with the these building blocks, and your meals will become faster to assemble, more balanced and delicious, while your time in the kitchen lessens.

USE YOUR FREEZER (NOT JUST FOR ICE CUBES!)

For many years my freezer was a storage space for ice pops and long-forgotten hunks of bread. Then I realized that it could be so much more . . . it's like a food time machine! Freezing cooked foods, especially beans and grains, is a perfectly respectable way to stretch your time and meals.

Here are a few things I always have on hand in my freezer and how long they can keep for:

- **cooked beans (6 months)**
- **cooked grains (6 months)**
- **frozen vegetables, like green peas (8 to 10 months)**
- **bread, wraps, muffins, other baked goods (6 months)**

HOW TO BOOST FLAVOR

Over many years of cooking, I've learned how to boost flavor in all kinds of food without the use of fancy equipment. The recipes in this book use all my favorite techniques, but I thought it would be fun to highlight them here to get you out of a cooking rut and get your own creative culinary juices flowing.

Grill and Char

If there is one technique to master it is this one. Grilling and charring food makes it delicious because of something called the Maillard Reaction. This complex process happens when sugars and amino acids in the food react to high heat, creating and releasing hundreds of potent molecules that enhance the taste of what you are eating. Sounds complicated, but all you need to do is turn up the heat and get cooking! Remember that what you're after is caramelization, not burnt food. A fine line, but an important one.

TRY IT: Charred Eggplant Baba Ganoush with Pine Nuts (page 167), Grilled Caesar Salad with Chickpea Croutons (page 61)

Toast

In line with grilling and charring, toasting also creates the Maillard Reaction, giving us the same food with a more intense flavor. The foods that benefit the most from toasting are nuts, seeds, spices, grains, and of course bread. You can toast almost anything in a pan, but the slower and most effective way is actually in the oven. With odd-shaped ingredients like walnuts, a pan is only going to deliver heat to the parts of the food that it touches, usually creating burnt spots while the rest of the ingredient remains raw. In the oven you can surround the food with heat, creating an evenly toasted product that tastes really amazing. The only drawback with the oven is that you can't keep an eye on the food, so take the pan out of the oven often to prevent burning.

TRY IT: Toasted Walnut Sauce (page 84), Honey Almond Granola Bars (page 218)

Roast

A tried-and-true cooking method, this is one I use a *lot*. And not just for vegetables—fruit and cheese get the lovin' oven treatment too. The process of roasting helps the liquid to evaporate in the food you're cooking, which in turn intensifies the natural flavors. Sugars caramelize and sharp tastes mellow into something sweeter and more palatable.

TRY IT: Roasted Radishes and Avocado with Sesame Salt (page 157), Balsamic-Roasted Plums with Spinach and Goat Cheese (page 70)

Marinate or Infuse

This technique relies on an intensely flavored combination of spices, herbs, and seasoning to bathe your food in. This infuses the food with major taste. You can cook the food afterward or leave it raw. Sometimes I recommend placing the food in the marinade after cooking, while it is still warm, which helps the food absorb even more flavor.

TRY IT: Marinated Roasted Red Peppers with Chickpeas (page 164), Portobello Pizzas (page 119)

Seasoning with Salt

Sometimes an extra pinch of salt can mean the difference between a plain dish and a really yummy one. If you feel like something is missing, try adding a little salt first and see if it makes a difference—especially in sweet foods and desserts (trust me on this). Salt your food in small increments as you cook, tasting as you go. My recipes tend to be less salty than what most people are used to, so you can salt food to suit your preference.

TRY IT: Broccoli with Garlic Ghee and Pine Nuts (page 171), Brilliant Banana Almond Soft-Serve (page 221)

Add a Little Acid

If you ask most professional chefs what is missing in home-cooked meals, they will almost always say "acid." Acidity gives food sourness, brightness, and tang, but most importantly, balance! There are two ways to add acidity to food: citrus (lemon or lime juice) or vinegar (I love apple cider vinegar). Pickles are a fabulous complement to many dishes, and it doesn't require much acidity to take your food from flat to fab; if you ever go overboard with the acid, add something sugary (for example, pure maple syrup) or fatty (for example, cold-pressed olive oil) to even things out.

TRY IT: Lemony Raw Beet and Quinoa Salad with Dill and Olives (page 91), Pico de Gallo (page 112)

Finish with Fat

Fat tastes good. In fact we are biologically hardwired to like the taste of fat because it is the densest form of energy out there, and for a long time our survival depended on it. Fat also helps us to feel satisfied—and thus it's an important aspect in any dish. We feel fuller longer by eating fats and oils because they take longer to digest, which is one reason that low-fat diets often fail—people tend to feel hungry soon after consuming low-fat foods. Because fruits and vegetables are relatively low in fat, most of my recipes are too. So I will often suggest drizzling the finished dish with olive oil, which not only delivers richness and creamy texture, but satiety as well.

TRY IT: Divine and Foolproof Mayonnaise (page 111), Brown Butter Carrots with Pistachios and Dill (page 163)

Garnish Before Serving

Adding edibles with tons of taste as you are finishing up the preparation and cooking is not really a technique, but it's an important way to increase the personality in foods. It's what will prompt your friends to exclaim, "Wow! How did you make this?" and make you feel like a pro. Some of my favorite garnishes are fresh herbs, capers, olives, red pepper flakes, citrus zest, toasted nuts and seeds, toasted coconut, spice blends, infused oil, and nori flakes. Having one or more of these elements in your kitchen at all times gives you flavor superpowers.

TRY IT: So-Simple Roasted Roots with Dukkah (page 183), Sesame Salt (page 157)

satisfying
SOUPS

———

———

PREVIOUS PAGE, from left to right: Spring Minestrone, page 17 / Summer Minestrone, page 18 /
Fall Minestrone, page 19

MINESTRONE, 3 WAYS

Minestrone is a classic, fully-loaded Italian vegetable soup. Since it is typically made with seasonal ingredients, I took liberties and created three recipes—one each for spring, summer, and fall. Each of these soups tastes remarkably different, but all begin with oil, onion, salt, and garlic, then veer off to wherever the season wills it. I love adding beans to give the soups more body and satiety, but lentils would also work well. If you do not want to add pasta to your soup, try using a julienne peeler to make noodles out of seasonal veggies, as I do in the summer version. *Buon appetito!*

2 tablespoons fine sea salt

1 cup / 100g dried gluten-free or whole-grain shell pasta of your choice

1 tablespoon coconut oil or ghee

3 medium yellow onions, diced

3 garlic cloves, minced

4 spring onions, white and green parts, sliced

7 cups / 1.75 liters vegetable broth

1 cup / 150g green peas, fresh or frozen

½ pound / 225g asparagus, chopped

3½ ounces / 100g snow peas, chopped

1½ cups / 225g (1 15-oz. can) cooked butter beans

2 packed cups / 150g chopped Swiss chard

½ packed cup / 15g chopped fresh flat-leaf parsley

1 teaspoon freshly ground black pepper

1 tablespoon freshly squeezed lemon juice

Cold-pressed olive oil, for serving

SPRING MINESTRONE

SERVES 6 TO 8 ────────────────────────

1 Fill a medium saucepan with water and bring to a boil. Add 1½ teaspoons of the sea salt and the pasta, and cook until al dente, according to the directions on the package. Drain and set aside.

2 In a large stockpot, melt the coconut oil over medium heat. Add the yellow onions and remaining 1½ tablespoons of salt and stir to coat. Cook, stirring occasionally, until the onions soften and begin to slightly caramelize, about 10 minutes.

3 Add the garlic, spring onions, and broth, and bring to a boil. Add the green peas, asparagus, snow peas, and butter beans, and cook until the peas are bright green, 3 to 4 minutes.

4 Remove from the heat, add the Swiss chard, parsley, black pepper, and lemon juice. Stir to wilt the chard.

5 Add the cooked pasta immediately before serving. Season with salt. Serve hot with a drizzle of cold-pressed olive oil.

1 tablespoon coconut oil
or ghee

3 medium yellow onions,
diced

1 teaspoon fine sea salt

3 garlic cloves, minced

4 celery stalks, diced

1 red bell pepper (stem,
seeds, and ribs removed),
diced

3½ ounces / 100g green
beans, chopped

1 pound / 500g tomatoes,
diced

6 cups vegetable broth

1½ cups / 225g (1 15-oz.
can) cooked chickpeas,
drained and rinsed

1 small zucchini, sliced
with a julienne peeler or
spiralizer into long, thin
strips, like spaghetti

½ packed cup / 7g fresh
basil leaves

1 teaspoon freshly ground
black pepper

Cold-pressed olive oil, for
serving

SUMMER MINESTRONE

SERVES 6 TO 8 ——————————————————————

1 In a large stockpot, melt the coconut oil over medium heat. Add the onions and salt and stir to coat. Cook, stirring occasionally, until the onions soften and begin to slightly caramelize, about 10 minutes.

2 Add the garlic, celery, bell pepper, green beans, and tomatoes. Stir to coat and cook until fragrant, about 5 minutes.

3 Add the broth, bring to a boil, then reduce the heat to low and simmer until the vegetables are tender, about 10 minutes.

4 Remove from the heat and add the chickpeas, zucchini, and basil. Season with black pepper and serve with a drizzle of olive oil.

FALL MINESTRONE

SERVES 6 TO 8

1 Fill a medium saucepan with water and bring to a boil. Add 1½ teaspoons of the sea salt and the pasta and cook according to the package instructions until al dente. Drain and set aside.

2 In a large stockpot, melt the coconut oil over medium heat. Add the onions and remaining 1½ tablespoons of salt and stir to coat. Cook, stirring occasionally, until the onions soften and begin to slightly caramelize, about 10 minutes.

3 Add the garlic, rosemary, thyme, leeks, pumpkin, and carrots. Stir to coat and cook until the herbs are fragrant, about 5 minutes.

4 Add the broth, bring to a boil, then reduce the heat to low and simmer until the pumpkin and carrots are tender, about 20 minutes.

5 Remove from the heat and add the kidney beans, spinach, black pepper, and cooked pasta. Serve hot with a drizzle of olive oil.

2 tablespoons fine sea salt

1 cup / 100g dried gluten-free or whole-grain corkscrew pasta of your choice

1 tablespoon coconut oil or ghee

3 medium red onions

3 garlic cloves

2 tablespoons chopped fresh rosemary

1 tablespoon fresh thyme leaves

3 leeks, white and light-green parts, chopped

3½ cups / 400g chopped pumpkin

5 medium carrots, chopped

8 cups / 2 liters vegetable broth

1½ cups / 250g (1 15-oz. can) cooked kidney beans, drained and rinsed

2 packed cups / 60g spinach or kale

1 teaspoon freshly ground black pepper

Cold-pressed olive oil, for serving

PANTRY PEA AND DILL SOUP

When I was in school studying holistic nutrition, I had so little time to cook and eat healthfully that my studies versus my habits became a bit of a joke—but not one that I was laughing at! To remedy my feelings of utter hypocrisy, I came up with this wholesome and quick-to-make soup to power me through all-night study sessions. It continues to be one of my favorite meals, because I can keep all of the ingredients on hand, since the recipe uses frozen peas and dried dill. You can of course use fresh in both cases, but for anyone with a busy lifestyle, this is the ultimate convenience food. Even today, my Pantry Pea and Dill Soup usually ends up as dinner when there is "nothing to eat" in the house.

SERVES 4 ───────────────────────────

Knob of coconut oil or ghee

2 medium yellow onions

Fine sea salt

3 garlic cloves

16 ounces / 500g frozen green peas

3 cups / 750ml hot vegetable broth

1 tablespoon dried dill

Zest of 1 lemon

1 tablespoon freshly squeezed lemon juice, plus more as needed

Cold-pressed olive oil, for serving

1 In a medium saucepan, heat the coconut oil over medium heat. Add the onions and a pinch of salt. Cook until the onions have softened, about 5 minutes. Add the garlic and stir, cooking for 2 minutes more.

2 Add the peas and vegetable broth. Cook just until the peas are bright green and no longer frozen, 1 to 2 minutes only.

3 Quickly but carefully ladle the soup into a blender. Add the dill, lemon zest, and juice. Blend on high until completely smooth. Taste and adjust the seasoning, if necessary.

4 Transfer the soup to a saucepan and heat until hot. Serve with a drizzle of olive oil.

ROLLOVER Use any leftover soup in the Cool It Noodle Salad with Radishes and Peas (page 104) instead of the Spicy Tahini Ginger Sauce—it will change up the flavor profile and create a totally different and delicious dish!

SPROUTED MUNG BEAN GAZPACHO

9 ounces / 250g cherry tomatoes

1 medium cucumber

1 red bell pepper, stem, seeds, and ribs removed

1 cup / 60g mung bean sprouts (recipe follows)

2 tablespoons cold-pressed olive oil, plus more for drizzling

½ teaspoon fine sea salt, plus more as needed

1.7 pounds / 750g Roma tomatoes

1 garlic clove

½ teaspoon freshly ground black pepper, plus more as needed

1 tablespoon freshly squeezed lemon juice

1 tablespoon freshly squeezed lime juice

1 to 2 teaspoons apple cider vinegar, plus more if desired

Grilled crusty whole-grain bread, for serving (optional)

Gazpacho is *the* classic summer soup, but I've changed things up a little by adding mung bean sprouts to deliver a totally unique flavor and texture. As a bonus, you'll be getting far more protein, fiber, and phytonutrients.

Because produce varies so widely according to seasonality and availability, this recipe should be used more as a guide than as a strict prescription. I find that playing with the salt and acidity levels is important to the success of this soup, so up the salt and vinegar until you achieve a tasty balance that suits your palate.

Any sprouts will work here if you don't have mung beans; just remember that sprouts take about three days to grow, so start this recipe ahead of time!

SERVES 4

1 Finely dice half the cherry tomatoes, half the cucumber, and half the bell pepper.

2 In a medium bowl, combine the diced vegetables with the mung bean sprouts, a drizzle of olive oil, and a pinch of salt. Stir and set aside.

3 Roughly chop the Roma tomatoes and place them in a blender with the remaining cherry tomatoes, cucumber, and bell pepper, plus the garlic, ½ teaspoon of salt, black pepper, 2 tablespoons oil, citrus juices, and vinegar. Blend on high until smooth. Taste and adjust the flavors.

4 Transfer the gazpacho to a large serving bowl and add almost all of the diced vegetable–mung bean mixture, reserving a few spoonfuls for garnish. Place in the fridge to chill for at least 1 hour to allow the flavors to meld.

5 Ladle the soup into bowls and top with the remaining diced vegetable–mung bean mixture. Serve with the grilled whole-grain bread.

ROLLOVER Sprout extra mung beans to make the Sprouted Mung Bean and Mango Avocado Cups (page 67).

BASIC SPROUTS

MAKES 1 CUP

I go into more detail about sprouting on my blog, but it's really a simple process.

(V) (GF) (R) (GrF)

2 tablespoons seeds, beans, or lentils

1 Place the seeds in a clean glass jar and fill it almost to the top with water. Cover the jar with a piece of screen and secure it with a rubber band. Let the seeds soak at room temperature for 8 to 12 hours, or overnight.

2 Drain and rinse the seeds through the screen 2 or 3 times. Set the jar upside down at a 45° angle in a bowl or dish rack to drain completely. Keep the seeds away from light or cover the glass with a clean kitchen towel.

3 Repeat the rinsing and draining upside down at a 45° angle 2 or 3 times daily for 2 to 4 days until the seeds grow a good tail (at least 2 times longer than the seed itself).

4 Once the seeds have sprouted to your liking, rinse and drain the sprouts completely and let them sit out in a colander for at least 8 hours before adding them back to the jar, covering with an airtight lid, and storing them in the fridge for up to 2 weeks.

CHILL-OUT CUCUMBER AND AVOCADO SOUP

with Mint and Dukkah

2 English cucumbers, roughly chopped

2 ripe avocados, flesh scooped out

3 tablespoons freshly squeezed lemon juice

⅔ packed cup / 15g fresh mint leaves

1 teaspoon fine sea salt

1 tablespoon cold-pressed olive oil

¼ cup / 12g chopped fresh chives

¼ cup / 7g chopped fresh flat-leaf parsley

1 cup / 250ml water

Dukkah, for serving (optional; recipe follows)

When summertime hits, I miss soup like a long-lost friend. This year, I decided to chill out and find a new solution besides my beloved gazpacho (page 22), and I came up with this incredible concoction. Creamy avocado and crisp cucumber make the most amazing blend, especially when combined with lemon and mint. Dukkah—an Egyptian herb, nut, and spice mixture—is the ideal accompaniment, grounding a dish that is otherwise raw and quite light. Sesame Salt (page 157) would also be delicious with this soup. If your blender is not very powerful, try straining the soup through a sieve to achieve extra smoothness.

SERVES 3 TO 4

1 In a blender, combine the cucumbers, avocados, lemon juice, mint leaves, salt, oil, chives, parsley, and water, and blend on high until the mixture is as smooth as possible. Strain through a fine sieve for extra smoothness, if desired. Season with salt.

2 Place in the fridge to chill for at least 2 hours to allow the flavors to meld. Enjoy cold, topped with Dukkah, if desired.

ROLLOVER Use the leftover Dukkah for the So-Simple Roasted Roots with Dukkah (page 183).

(recipe continues)

(V) (GF) (GrF)

1 cup / 140g raw, unsalted hazelnuts

1 tablespoon coriander seeds

1½ teaspoons cumin seeds

1 tablespoon whole black peppercorns

½ cup / 75g raw, unsalted sesame seeds

1 teaspoon fine sea salt, plus more as needed

DUKKAH

MAKES ABOUT 1 CUP / 225G

1 Preheat the oven to 325°F / 160°C. Spread the hazelnuts out in a single layer on a rimmed baking sheet and roast until fragrant and the skins have turned darker in color, 20 to 30 minutes. (Another good way to check for doneness is to bite a hazelnut in half and inspect the color— it should be golden, not white, inside.) Remove from the oven, and when cool enough to handle, rub the nuts together to remove the skins. Place the nuts in a food processor.

2 While the hazelnuts are roasting, preheat a dry skillet over medium heat. When hot, toast the coriander and cumin seeds, stirring often, until fragrant, about 2 minutes. Remove the pan from the heat immediately, let the seeds cool, then place them in a mortar and pestle and add the peppercorns. Using the pestle, grind the seeds and peppercorns together until pulverized. (Alternatively, grind them together in a coffee mill or food processor.) Set aside.

3 In the same skillet, toast the sesame seeds until they are fragrant and begin to pop, about 2 minutes. Let cool slightly. Place the sesame seeds in the food processor with the hazelnuts. Pulse to chop the mixture until you get a chunky-sand texture. (Do not blend, or you will end up with hazelnut-sesame butter! Tasty, but not what we're after.)

4 Add the pulverized spices and the salt to the food processor and pulse once more to combine. Taste and adjust the seasonings, if necessary. Store in an airtight glass container at room temperature for up to 1 month.

LUXURIOUS CREAM OF MUSHROOM SOUP

with Garlic-Herb Croutons

The only cream of mushroom soup I ate as a kid was the canned variety—the one that plopped out of its claustrophobic aluminum home and retained its cylindrical-tin shape. You know the one I mean.

These days, I still love mushroom soup, but I make it from scratch without dairy. What is the secret to the creaminess without the cream? By blending cooked beans with vegetable broth, you end up with a totally luxurious texture that mimics heavy cream but is virtually fat free. In addition, beans deliver healthy, vegetarian protein and a serious dose of filling fiber. It tastes as if you are eating the richest soup of all time, but it's a delicious illusion that warms you up, fills you up, but doesn't fill you out!

To take this delicious soup to the next level, you *must* make the Garlic-Herb Croutons. They are ridiculously rich, perfectly seasoned, and extra crunchy. You'll be finding reasons to make soup just to eat them!

SERVES 4 ——————————————————

1 To prepare the leeks, cut the white and light-green parts in half lengthwise and then crosswise into chunks.

2 In a large stockpot, melt the coconut oil over medium heat. Add the onions, leeks, salt, black pepper, thyme, and bay leaves. Cook until the onions and leeks are soft, about 5 minutes. Mince the garlic, add it to the pot, and stir.

3 While the onions, leeks, and garlic are cooking, clean the mushrooms by removing any dirt or natural debris with a damp cloth (do not wash them in water). Cut the mushrooms into quarters and add them to the pot. Cook until they are dark brown and very soft, 10 to 15 minutes. Add the broth and stir.

1 large leek

1 tablespoon coconut oil or ghee

3 medium yellow onions, chopped

1 teaspoon fine sea salt, plus more as needed

1 teaspoon freshly ground black pepper, plus more as needed

2 teaspoons fresh thyme leaves (or 1 teaspoon dried), plus more for garnish

4 bay leaves

4 garlic cloves

14 ounces / 400g cremini mushrooms

2 cups / 500ml vegetable broth

1 cup / 250ml plant-based milk of your choice

1½ cups / 250g (about 1 15-oz. can) white beans, such as navy, butter, cannellini, or great Northern, drained and rinsed

1½ teaspoons balsamic vinegar

Garlic-Herb Croutons (recipe follows)

(recipe continues)

4 Meanwhile, combine the milk and beans in a blender and blend on high until smooth.

5 When the mushrooms are cooked, add the vinegar and about one third of the soup to the blender with the blended beans. Blend on high until creamy, then pour the mixture back into the pot with the remaining soup, stir well, and reduce the heat to low. Simmer for 5 minutes. Thin the soup with water if desired.

6 Season with plenty of freshly ground black pepper and sea salt. Ladle the soup into bowls and sprinkle with the croutons and some fresh thyme sprigs.

ROLLOVER Make extra croutons and use them for the Grilled Caesar Salad instead of the chickpea croutons (page 61).

GARLIC-HERB CROUTONS

MAKES 4 CUPS

1 Preheat the oven to 325°F / 160°C.

2 In a small saucepan, melt the coconut oil over medium heat. Add the garlic and onion powders, thyme, oregano, and salt, whisking to combine.

3 Place the bread cubes on a rimmed baking sheet and pour the oil mixture over the top, tossing very well to coat the bread. Bake until the croutons are golden, fully toasted, and dry, 35 to 45 minutes. Store leftovers in an airtight glass jar at room temperature for up 2 weeks.

1½ teaspoons coconut oil

½ teaspoon garlic powder

½ teaspoon onion powder

¼ teaspoon dried thyme

¼ teaspoon dried oregano

¼ teaspoon fine sea salt

4 cups / 330g cubed whole-grain bread (sourdough, if possible)

NORTH AFRICAN SUN-DRIED TOMATO SOUP

with Couscous Topping

SOUP

1 tablespoon coconut oil
or ghee

3 medium yellow onions,
chopped

2 pinches of fine sea salt

3 garlic cloves, minced

2 teaspoons ground cumin

1 teaspoon ground
cinnamon

2 teaspoons ground
coriander

1 tablespoon peeled, minced
fresh ginger

1 tablespoon gluten-free
harissa paste (available
at Middle Eastern grocery
stores)

2 large red bell peppers
(stems, seeds, and ribs
removed), chopped

5 to 6 cups / 1.25 to
1.5 liters vegetable broth

1 14.5-oz. / 400ml can
whole tomatoes

1 cup / 100g chopped
sun-dried tomatoes

1½ cups / 225g (1 15-oz.
can) cooked chickpeas,
drained and rinsed

This hearty dish is a perfect meal to enjoy when the first autumn days are creeping in and you need a little coziness, but you can also enjoy it cold. By using a combination of sun-dried and canned tomatoes, you'll add tons of umami notes to a totally vegan soup. The texture of the couscous topping provides a welcoming contrast to the smooth purée, while the olives lend a salty bite and the parsley adds a fresh note. Harissa is a Tunisian hot chile paste. It's easy to make (the recipe is on the *My New Roots* blog!), or look for it premade at the grocery store. If you do not have harissa paste, simply add some cayenne pepper or smoked hot paprika, as desired.

SERVES 4 TO 6

1 Start the soup: In a large stockpot, melt the coconut oil over medium heat. Add the onions and salt and stir to coat. Cook, stirring occasionally, until the onions soften and begin to slightly caramelize, about 10 minutes. Add the garlic, cumin, cinnamon, coriander, ginger, and harissa paste and cook until fragrant, about 2 minutes. Add the bell peppers and cook for 5 minutes, adding a little broth to the pot if the mixture becomes dry.

2 Add the whole tomatoes and their juices along with the sun-dried tomatoes and the rest of the broth. Bring to a boil, reduce the heat to low, and cook for 15 minutes.

3 Carefully transfer the soup to a blender and blend on high until smooth. Return the soup to the pot, add the chickpeas, and heat through.

4 Meanwhile, make the couscous topping: In a small pot, combine the couscous and the salt, and cook according to the package directions. Fluff with a fork, then add the olives, parsley, lemon zest and juice, and olive oil. Season with salt.

5 To serve, ladle the soup into bowls and top with as much couscous as desired. Enjoy hot or cold.

ROLLOVER Use extra sun-dried tomatoes in the Smoked Lentil Tacos with Pico de Gallo (page 112).

COUSCOUS TOPPING

½ cup / 90g whole wheat couscous

¼ teaspoon fine sea salt

½ cup / 75g chopped black olives

½ cup / 13g chopped fresh flat-leaf parsley

Zest of 1 lemon

1½ teaspoons freshly squeezed lemon juice

1 tablespoon olive oil

GINGER-LEMON
SPLIT PEA SOUP

My father-in-law is obsessed with traditions. Birthdays, holidays, weddings, graduations . . . he's there to make the day special and momentous, and, of course, to remind us all of the elaborate ways we need to carry out the proceedings *just* how everything was done the last time—because it's tradition. The last weekend in November, when all of Denmark is mourning the very last bits of light before winter, it is a tradition that we gather at my father-in-law's house for yellow split pea soup. For me, sitting around a long table with my large extended family, catching up over piping-hot bowls of golden soup is an antidote to the darkness and softens the blow of impending cold.

This is my version of the soup, which I continue to make from that weekend deep into the winter months to remedy whatever chill has taken hold. Split peas are relatively bland, so this soup relies on plenty of ginger and lemon for brightness, and pumpkin to bring sweetness and depth—certainly nontraditional but delicious additions. I like to crush a few pieces of the cooked pumpkin on the side of the pot with my wooden spoon and let it dissolve into the broth; it acts as a thickener and turns the soup a lovely golden hue.

SERVES 4 ————————

1 tablespoon coconut oil or ghee

3 medium yellow onions, diced

1 leek, white and light-green parts, chopped

1 teaspoon fine sea salt

5 garlic cloves, minced

3 tablespoons peeled, minced fresh ginger

1½ teaspoons ground turmeric

3 bay leaves

3 celery stalks, diced

1 pound / 500g pumpkin, chopped into cubes (sweet potatoes will also work)

1 cup / 200g yellow split peas, soaked if possible, drained and rinsed

6 cups / 1.5 liters vegetable broth

Freshly squeezed juice of 1 lemon, plus a few slices for garnish (optional)

1 In a large stockpot, melt the coconut oil over medium heat. Add the onions, leeks, and salt, and stir to coat. Cook, stirring occasionally, until the onions soften and begin to slightly caramelize, about 10 minutes. Add the garlic, ginger, turmeric, bay leaves, celery, pumpkin, and split peas. Toss to coat, then add the broth. Bring to a boil, reduce the heat to low, and simmer, covered, until the split peas and pumpkin are tender, 30 to 40 minutes.

2 Just before serving, add the lemon juice and season with salt. Ladle the soup into bowls and top with a slice of lemon, if using.

ROLLOVER If you have any leftover ginger, make the Ginger-Pickled Carrots (page 87).

GARLIC CLOUD SOUP

40 garlic cloves
(3 to 4 whole heads)

3 medium yellow onions

1 head of cauliflower

2 tablespoons coconut oil
or ghee, melted

1 teaspoon fine sea salt,
plus more as needed

2 cups / 500ml vegetable
broth

2 cups / 500ml plant-based
milk of your choice

1½ teaspoons freshly
squeezed lemon juice

Cold-pressed olive oil,
for serving

Let me start off by saying that, yes, this recipe calls for forty cloves of garlic and, no, I haven't totally lost my mind. This ethereally creamy, dreamy soup is for immune boosting and deep healing. Keep this recipe in your flu-busting arsenal, or whip some up right when you feel the sniffles coming on. Roasting the garlic this way really mellows out its sharpness, and I promise you can still be social after eating it!

SERVES 4

1 Preheat the oven to 400°F / 200°C.

2 Peel the garlic cloves and quarter the onions, and place them on a rimmed baking sheet. Cut up the cauliflower into bite-size chunks and add it to the garlic and onions. Drizzle with the melted coconut oil and toss to coat. Sprinkle with ½ teaspoon sea salt. Roast until everything has golden edges and is nicely caramelized, 25 to 30 minutes.

3 Let the veggies cool slightly and then add to a blender along with the vegetable broth, milk, remaining ½ teaspoon salt, and lemon juice (process in batches if you have a small blender). Blend on high until as smooth as possible. Taste and adjust the seasonings, if necessary.

4 If the soup is not hot enough after blending, transfer it to a large pot and warm until steaming. If the soup is too thick, simply add water to thin to your desired consistency. Serve hot with a drizzle of olive oil.

COCONUT ZINGER BLACK BEAN SOUP

1 tablespoon coconut oil

2 teaspoons ground cumin

1 teaspoon ground coriander

¼ teaspoon cayenne pepper

2 medium yellow onions, diced

½ teaspoon fine sea salt

5 garlic cloves, minced

1 heaping tablespoon peeled, minced fresh ginger

1 pound / 500g sweet potatoes (about 2 large), scrubbed and chopped

3 cups / 750ml vegetable broth or water

1 14-oz. / 400ml can full-fat coconut milk

3 cups / 500g (2 15-oz. cans) cooked black beans, drained and rinsed

2 to 3 tablespoons freshly squeezed lime juice

2 handfuls of fresh cilantro leaves and tender stems, chopped

Cold-pressed olive oil, for serving

ROLLOVER Cook extra black beans for the Quinoa and Black Beans with Radish Cilantro Salsa (page 106).

When you need something in your belly quick, this soup will not disappoint. With a couple of sweet potatoes, a can of coconut milk, and some cooked black beans that I had stashed in the freezer, I whipped this up so fast that I even shocked myself! The black beans and coconut are a surprising yet delightful combination, and, of course, with fiber-rich and tasty sweet potatoes we're all winners.

This soup needs a surprising amount of acid, in this case lime juice, to balance the sweetness of the coconut milk and sweet potatoes. Add it to your liking, and taste the results as you go. You can also make this as spicy as you like. The amount of cayenne I've indicated gives a medium heat level, but feel free to blow your head off.

SERVES 4 TO 6 ⸻

1 In a large stockpot, melt the coconut oil over medium heat. Add the cumin, coriander, and cayenne and cook, stirring constantly, until fragrant, about 2 minutes. Add the onions and salt, and stir to coat. Cook, stirring occasionally, until the onions have softened, 5 to 7 minutes.

2 Add the garlic and ginger and cook for 2 minutes; if the pot becomes dry at any point, add a little water or broth. Add the sweet potatoes, broth, and coconut milk.

3 Cover the pot and bring the soup to a boil, then reduce the heat to low and simmer until the potatoes are tender, 10 to 15 minutes. Add half of the black beans and simmer until they have warmed through.

4 Transfer about half of the soup to a blender and purée until completely smooth. Add the lime juice. Pour the blended soup back into the pot and add the remaining whole black beans. Season with salt. Serve hot, garnished with plenty of chopped cilantro and a drizzle of cold-pressed olive oil.

CASHEW CORN CHOWDER

with Chipotle Oil

1 tablespoon coconut oil
or ghee

1 tablespoon ground
turmeric

2 teaspoons ground cumin

2 pinches of cayenne pepper

3 medium yellow onions,
chopped

2 teaspoons fine sea salt,
plus more as needed

6 garlic cloves, minced

4 cups / 1 liter vegetable
broth

4 ears fresh corn

2/3 cup / 93g raw cashews,
soaked for at least 4 hours
or up to overnight

1 tablespoon freshly
squeezed lime juice

2 tablespoons cold-pressed
olive oil

1/4 teaspoon ground chipotle

Handful of fresh cilantro
leaves and tender stems, for
garnish

Classic chowder relies heavily on milk and cream, and perhaps a little butter for extra unctuousness. As yum as that is, if you have never used cashews to replace regular cream or milk in a soup before, I highly recommend you try it with this comfort food classic. I've also added a drizzle of chipotle oil for kick and a handful of herbaceous cilantro to take this soup to the next level. Spicy-Sweet Pumpkin Seed Snacks (page 211) sprinkled over the top would be delicious too.

SERVES 4

1 In a large pot, melt the coconut oil over medium heat. Add the turmeric, cumin, and cayenne, and cook until fragrant, about 1 minute. Add the onions and salt and cook until softened, about 5 minutes. Add the garlic. If the bottom of the pot becomes dry, add a little broth to moisten things up.

2 While the onions are cooking, cut off the kernels of the corn by standing each ear on its end in a shallow bowl and slicing downward. Add the corn kernels to the pot and stir to coat with the spices. Cook for 5 minutes, then add the remaining broth. Bring to a boil, then reduce the heat to low and simmer until the corn is bright yellow and sweet, about 5 minutes.

3 Once the corn is cooked, remove the pot from the heat and transfer the soup to a blender, reserving a few tablespoons of the whole corn kernels for garnish. Add the soaked and rinsed cashews and the lime juice. Blend on high until smooth. Add water to thin the soup if desired. Season with salt. If not serving right away, return the soup to the pot to keep warm.

4 In a small bowl, whisk the olive oil with the chipotle until thoroughly blended. Serve the soup with a drizzle of chipotle oil, a sprinkle of cilantro, and the reserved corn kernels.

ROLLOVER Use leftover cilantro for the
Radish Cilantro Salsa (page 108).

BROCCOLI BASIL BROTH

with Noodles and Sesame Salt

1 tablespoon plus
1 teaspoon fine sea salt

6 ounces / 170g dried
gluten-free or whole-grain
pasta of your choice

5 garlic cloves

1 tablespoon coconut oil
or ghee

3 medium yellow onions,
chopped

4 cups / 1 liter vegetable
broth

1 large head broccoli,
stalk removed and florets
separated

2 to 3 tablespoons freshly
squeezed lime juice

1 tablespoon pure maple
syrup

1 tablespoon peeled, minced
fresh ginger

1 cup / 25g basil leaves;
reserve a couple leaves for
garnish

Cold-pressed olive oil, for
serving

Sesame Salt (optional;
page 157)

If you're a parent, you'll understand the feeling of relief, accomplishment, and utter joy when your child eats something healthy. Although broccoli and basil don't seem like the most likely of pals, when my discriminating one-and-a-half-year-old son hoovers the combo, I am not going to argue. The secret to making broccoli taste great is not to overcook it, which brings out its sulfuric compounds. My method only allows the broccoli to bathe in hot broth for five minutes before a big blend-up, instead of boiling it to death.

SERVES 4

1 Fill a medium saucepan with water and bring to a boil. Add 1 tablespoon of the sea salt and the pasta, and cook until al dente, according to the package instructions. Drain and cover to keep warm.

2 Roughly chop and mince the garlic (no need to be too precise, since you'll be blending everything). In a large stockpot, melt the coconut oil over medium heat. Add the onions and remaining teaspoon of salt and stir to coat. Cook, stirring occasionally, until the onions soften and begin to slightly caramelize, about 10 minutes. Add the garlic and cook until fragrant, about 2 minutes.

3 Add the broth, bring to a boil, and reduce the heat to low. Add the broccoli, remove the pot from the heat, and let sit for 5 minutes.

4 Transfer the soup to a blender and blend on high until smooth. Add the lime juice, maple syrup, ginger, and basil leaves. Blend on high until incorporated. Season with salt.

5 Portion out the noodles into four bowls. Ladle the soup over top, garnish with basil, and drizzle with olive oil. Sprinkle with Sesame Salt, if desired.

ROLLOVER: Cook extra noodles to make the Cool It Noodle Salad with Radishes and Peas (page 104).

DEEP DETOX CILANTRO, SPINACH, AND SWEET POTATO SOUP

I originally created this recipe for a January detoxification post on my blog, but I love it so much that I make it all the time—even when I'm not on a cleanse! It is rich and hearty with tons of brightness from the lemon and cilantro, plus a little kick from the cayenne pepper. Even though it's super green, there is no flavor sacrifice here. Just another rad example of how food that tastes amazing can just "happen" to be healthy.

SERVES 4

1 In a large stockpot, melt the coconut oil over medium heat. Add the onions and salt, stir to coat, and cook until onions have softened, 5 to 7 minutes. Add the garlic, stir, and cook 1 minute more. Add the sweet potatoes and water. Bring the soup to a boil, then reduce the heat to low and simmer until the sweet potatoes are tender, 12 to 15 minutes.

2 Transfer the soup to a blender. Blend on high until smooth, then add the spinach, cilantro, lemon, and cayenne, and continue blending until smooth. Season with salt. Store cooled leftovers in the fridge for up to 3 days.

(V) (GF) (GrF)

1 tablespoon coconut oil

2 medium yellow onions, chopped

1 teaspoon fine sea salt

4 to 5 garlic cloves, minced (to suit your taste)

2 medium-large sweet potatoes, scrubbed and cut into 1-inch / 2.5cm cubes

3 cups / 750ml water

2 firmly packed cups / 50g fresh baby spinach

2 cups / 60g fresh cilantro leaves and tender stems

1 tablespoon freshly squeezed lemon juice

1 pinch to ¼ teaspoon cayenne pepper

RED VELVET ROASTED GARLIC BEET SOUP

with Mustard-Spiked Yogurt

2¼ pounds / 1kg beets

1 head of garlic

1 tablespoon plus ½ teaspoon coconut oil

3 leeks

1 teaspoon fine sea salt

2 teaspoons dried thyme

3 bay leaves

4 cups / 1 liter vegetable broth

1 tablespoon freshly squeezed lemon juice

½ teaspoon freshly ground black pepper

½ cup / 125g plain yogurt (preferably goat or sheep)

1 teaspoon Dijon mustard

ROLLOVER Roast extra beets for the Rainbow Hummus Bowl (page 74).

Roasting beets is a simple process that transforms the earthy, crunchy roots into silky, sweet, tender globes. Although you can steam and boil them, roasting concentrates their flavors and makes them much sweeter. I've taken advantage of the long cooking time to roast garlic too, which pairs so well with beets. Blended all together, this soup is so velvety.

SERVES 4 TO 6

1 Preheat the oven to 400°F / 200°C. Wrap each beet in foil and place them on a rimmed baking sheet. Slice off the portion just below the garlic bulb stem, revealing the cloves. Spread ½ teaspoon of the coconut oil on top, wrap the bulb in aluminum foil, and set on the baking sheet. Roast until the beets are tender when pierced with a knife, about 45 minutes.

2 Meanwhile, remove the dark-green tops of the leeks, slice the white and light-green parts in half lengthwise, and rinse well to remove any dirt. Slice the leeks crosswise into chunks.

3 In a large stockpot, melt the remaining 1 tablespoon of coconut oil over medium heat. Add the leeks and a few pinches of sea salt and stir. Add the thyme and bay leaves. Cook until the leeks soften, 5 minutes.

4 When the beets are roasted and are cool enough to handle, slip off their skins, cut them into chunks, and add them to the pot with the leeks. Add the broth, bring to a boil, reduce the heat to low, and simmer until the leeks are totally soft, 3 to 4 minutes.

5 Remove the foil from the garlic and squeeze the bulb from the bottom to extract the cloves directly into a blender. Discard the bay leaves from the pot. Add the beet mixture and lemon juice to the blender and mix on high until smooth. Season with salt and pepper. In a separate dish, stir the yogurt and mustard together, swirl into each bowl of soup, and enjoy.

GOLDEN CURRY COCONUT DAL

This soup was born at a restaurant where I worked called Morgenstedet (The Morning Place), which didn't make much sense because we opened at noon for lunch. We served vegetarian soups, salads, rice dishes, and casseroles—heartwarming homestyle food that drew large crowds every day of the year. I found the sheer quantity of food I had to make there incredibly daunting (I could quite literally sit in the soup pots!), and I was always pressed for time in the kitchen. This soup became my savior because it was so fast and easy to whip up, but it never tasted that way. In fact, on more occasions than I can count, people told me just how deep and delicious it was—I kept my secrets of simplicity to myself.

Double or triple the recipe—it tastes amazing the day after and freezes exceptionally well, or add more vegetables if you like: green peas, sweet potatoes, and pumpkin are especially tasty.

SERVES 4 ───────────────────────────────

1 tablespoon coconut oil or ghee

3 medium yellow onions, diced

2 teaspoons fine sea salt, plus more as needed

5 garlic cloves, minced

1 tablespoon peeled, minced fresh ginger

1 teaspoon ground cumin

1 tablespoon curry powder

1 teaspoon ground turmeric

3 cups / 750ml vegetable broth

1 cup / 200g red lentils, washed and drained

3 medium carrots, chopped

1 14.5-oz. / 400ml can whole tomatoes

1 14-oz. / 400ml can full-fat coconut milk

1 to 2 tablespoons freshly squeezed lime juice, plus more as needed

Handful of fresh cilantro leaves and tender stems, for serving

1 In a large stockpot, melt the coconut oil over medium-high heat. Add the onions and salt, stir to coat, and cook until the onions soften and begin to slightly caramelize, about 10 minutes.

2 Add the garlic, ginger, cumin, curry powder, and turmeric. Stir well and cook until fragrant, about 3 minutes, adding a little broth to the pot if it becomes too dry.

3 Add the lentils, carrots, tomatoes, coconut milk, and remaining broth. Bring to a boil, reduce the heat to low, and simmer until the lentils are tender, about 20 minutes. If the tomatoes remain whole after cooking, give them a squish against the side of the pot with a spoon to break them up a little.

4 Just before serving, stir in the lime juice, a little at a time, until the flavors are to your liking. Season with salt and serve with the cilantro.

CLEVER PARSNIP OVEN SOUP

1 small head of garlic

½ teaspoon coconut oil or ghee

2 pounds / 1kg parsnips

3 medium yellow onions

6 cups / 1.5 liters vegetable broth or water

1½ cups / 250g (about 1 15.5-oz. can) white beans, such as cannellini, great Northern, or navy, drained and rinsed

1 to 2 teaspoons fine sea salt (use 1 teaspoon if using broth; 2 teaspoons if using water)

1 tablespoon cold-pressed olive oil, plus more for serving

1 tablespoon freshly squeezed lemon juice

Freshly ground black pepper, for serving

The process for this soup is incredibly easy: all the ingredients are placed on a rimmed baking sheet, and the oven does the work. There isn't even a pot to wash when the meal's over. You can use this procedure with any veggies, plus onions and garlic. Just add everything to a blender directly from the oven, pour in some hot vegetable broth, and dinner is served. Bam!

SERVES 6

1 Preheat the oven to 400°F / 200°C. Slice off the stem of the garlic bulb and the portion just below the stem, revealing the open cloves. Spread the coconut oil on top, wrap the bulb tightly in aluminum foil, and set it on a rimmed baking sheet. Roast for 15 minutes.

2 While the garlic is roasting, peel and roughly cut the parsnips into similarly sized chunks to ensure even roasting. Chop the onions. After the garlic has roasted for 15 minutes, add the parsnips and onions to the baking sheet. Roast until tender, about 30 minutes.

3 Place the roasted parsnips and onions in a blender. Remove the foil from the garlic and squeeze the bulb from the bottom to extract the cloves into the blender. Add the broth, beans, salt, olive oil, and lemon juice, and blend on the highest setting until the soup is smooth and creamy. Transfer the soup to a stockpot and heat until steaming, if necessary.

4 Serve hot with a drizzle of olive oil and some black pepper.

sumptuous
SALADS
—

PREVIOUS PAGE, from left to right: Roasted Sweet Potato and Butter Beans on Massaged Kale, page 54 / Massaged Kale Pressed Salad, page 56 / Harissa-Dressed Massaged Kale, page 55

MASSAGED KALE, 3 WAYS

In recent years we've seen a maniacal surge in the popularity of fermented foods, coconut water, and "putting an egg on it," but the biggest trend of all is kale. It seems as if every restaurant menu and every cookbook and food blog (including mine) has incorporated the king of green—and who's complaining? Certainly not me! Trends can be silly, sure, but this is one craze I can get behind. My favorite way to enjoy kale is by massaging it, which turns kale into a delicate, tender, dark-green delight that will keep well in the fridge for up to a week.

Here, too, is a recipe for a pressed salad, which is a classic macrobiotic technique that uses salt to help break down some of the hard-to-digest fibers of the vegetables. After massaging the vegetables, which releases their water, you press them down with a plate to mix the water with the salt, which essentially dresses the salad, so you don't need any other sauce besides a light squeeze of lemon, if you wish. Pressed salads are easy to make, versatile, and incredibly delicious! Change up the ingredients to suit the season. These recipes are my love letter to massaged kale—three ways to take this tender, verdant base in different directions.

ROLLOVER Massage extra kale to use in Ceremonial Stuffed Pumpkin with Bulgur, Feta, and Figs (page 143).

SALAD

1 large sweet potato

1 teaspoon coconut oil, melted

¾ teaspoon fine sea salt, plus more as needed

4 packed cups / 120g shredded curly kale (shredding how-to included)

1 tablespoon cold-pressed olive oil, plus more as needed

1 tablespoon freshly squeezed lemon juice

1 small red onion, thinly sliced

⅓ cup / 45g raw, unsalted pumpkin seeds

1½ cups / 225g (1 15-oz. can) butter beans, drained and rinsed

LEMON GARLIC DRESSING

1 small garlic clove, finely minced

2 tablespoons cold-pressed olive oil

Zest of 1 lemon

2 tablespoons freshly squeezed lemon juice

Pinch of fine sea salt

¼ to ½ teaspoon pure maple syrup or raw honey

ROASTED SWEET POTATO AND BUTTER BEANS
on Massaged Kale

SERVES 4 AS A MAIN, 6 AS A SIDE ————————————

1 Prepare the salad: Preheat the oven to 400°F / 200°C. Peel the sweet potato (if it's not organic) and cut it into cubes. Place the cubes on a rimmed baking sheet and toss with the melted coconut oil and ¼ teaspoon of sea salt. Roast until tender, 15 to 20 minutes. Let cool and then put the cubes into a large bowl or serving platter.

2 Meanwhile, wash the kale well and spin it dry. Remove the stems and tough ribs, roll the leaves into a cigar shape, and slice crosswise to make ribbons. In a large bowl, combine the kale ribbons with the olive oil, ½ teaspoon of salt, and the lemon juice. Using your hands, rub and squeeze the kale together as if you are giving it a massage, until the kale leaves are dark green and tender, about 2 minutes. Add the kale to the sweet potato cubes. Sprinkle the onion slices over the top.

3 Preheat a small dry skillet over medium heat. When hot, toast the pumpkin seeds, tossing often, until fragrant, 3 to 5 minutes. Remove the pan from the heat immediately, let the seeds cool, then crush them with a mortar and pestle, if desired (crushed seeds add a nice texture to the salad).

4 Make the dressing: In a small bowl, whisk together the garlic, olive oil, lemon zest and juice, salt, and maple syrup.

5 Finish the salad: Place the beans in a medium bowl. Pour half of the dressing over the beans, stir well to coat, and let them marinate for 5 to 10 minutes. Add the marinated beans to the kale, sweet potato, and red onion. Pour the remaining dressing over the top, sprinkle with the pumpkin seeds, and serve.

HARISSA-DRESSED MASSAGED KALE

SERVES 4 AS A MAIN, 6 AS A SIDE ───────────

1 Prepare the salad: Wash the kale well and spin it dry. Remove the stems and tough ribs, roll the leaves into a cigar shape, and slice crosswise to make ribbons. In a large bowl, combine the kale ribbons with the olive oil, salt, and lemon juice. Using your hands, rub and squeeze the kale together as if you are giving it a massage, until the kale leaves are dark green and tender, about 2 minutes.

2 Make the dressing: In a small bowl, whisk together the harissa, olive oil, lemon juice, maple syrup, and salt.

3 Finish the salad: Using a vegetable peeler or mandoline slicer, slice the carrots lengthwise into long, thin ribbons. Add the carrots, feta, and raisins to the kale. Pour the dressing over the top, lightly toss the ingredients together, and serve.

SALAD

8 packed cups / 240g shredded curly kale (shredding how-to included)

2 tablespoons cold-pressed olive oil

½ teaspoon fine sea salt

2 tablespoons freshly squeezed lemon juice

2 large carrots

3½ ounces / 100g feta (preferably goat or sheep), crumbled

¼ cup / 35g raisins, roughly chopped

HARISSA DRESSING

4 teaspoons gluten-free harissa paste (available at Middle Eastern grocery stores)

3 tablespoons cold-pressed olive oil

2 teaspoons freshly squeezed lemon juice

¼ teaspoon pure maple syrup or raw honey

Pinch of fine sea salt

V | GF | R | GrF

4 packed cups / 240g shredded curly kale (shredding how-to included)

2 pounds / 1kg mixed vegetables (I recommend ½ small head red, 1 large carrot, 1 small sweet potato, 1 small fennel bulb, and 1 small red onion)

1 small apple

1½ teaspoons peeled, minced fresh ginger

2 teaspoons fine sea salt

Juice of 1 lemon

FOR SERVING

Handful of fresh flat-leaf parsley

Handful of fresh cilantro leaves and tender stems

Sesame Salt (optional; page 157)

Lemon wedges

Cold-pressed olive oil

MASSAGED KALE PRESSED SALAD

SERVES 4 AS A MAIN, 6 AS A SIDE ———————————————

1 Prepare the salad: Wash the kale and cabbage leaves well and spin them dry. Remove stems and tough ribs, roll the leaves into a cigar shape and slice them crosswise to make ribbons. Combine them in a large bowl.

2 Using a julienne slicer (or good knife skills!), julienne the carrot, sweet potato, fennel, red onion, and apple. Add the vegetables and ginger to the cabbage and kale. Sprinkle the salt over top.

3 Using your hands, rub and squeeze everything together as if you are giving it a massage, until the vegetables begin to break down and release a great deal of their liquid when you squeeze a large handful. If there is not a lot of liquid, keep massaging.

4 Press the salad: Place a plate directly on top of the massaged vegetables and weight it down with a heavy object, such as a quart jar filled with water. Let the salad press for about 30 minutes.

5 Finish the salad: Just before serving, fold the lemon juice in the vegetables. Chop the parsley and cilantro. Divide the salad among individual plates and sprinkle each portion with fresh herbs and Sesame Salt, if using. Serve with lemon wedges and olive oil. Once made, this salad keeps very well in the fridge for a few days.

SNAPPY SPRING SALAD

with Lemon-Mint Date Sauce

I was recently catching up with an old friend who told me that her absolute favorite recipe on my blog was the Snappy Spring Salad, which is from a post so old that I had long forgotten about it. But her enthusiasm had me intrigued: what was it about this simple-sounding salad that was so darn delish? So I tried it again. And then I remembered. This is exactly what I feel like when the winter frost retreats and weather turns warm enough for things to grow again. It tastes fresh and alive, especially with the Lemon-Mint Date Sauce, which is unreasonably delicious.

SERVES 4 AS A MAIN, 6 AS A SIDE

1 Make the quinoa: Rinse the quinoa well. In a small saucepan, combine the quinoa, water, and salt. Bring to a boil, reduce the heat to low, and cook, covered, until all the water has been absorbed and the grains are tender, about 20 minutes. Fluff with a fork.

2 Prepare the vegetables: Meanwhile, bring a pot of water to a boil. Add the peas and cook until they are bright green, 1 to 2 minutes. Quickly drain and run under cold water to halt the cooking. Wash the asparagus and snap off the thick ends where they naturally break. Using a vegetable peeler, slice the asparagus lengthwise into long, thin ribbons.

3 Toast the seeds: Preheat a dry skillet over medium heat. When hot, toast the pumpkin seeds, tossing often, until fragrant, 3 to 5 minutes. Remove the pan from the heat immediately and set aside.

4 Finish the salad: Slice the radishes on the bias. In a large bowl, combine the cooked quinoa with the radishes, peas, asparagus, and pumpkin seeds. Pour in about half of the sauce, season with a couple of pinches of fine sea salt, and toss well. Taste and add more sauce if you like. Finish with a pinch or two of flaky sea salt.

QUINOA

1 cup / 170g quinoa, soaked if possible

1¾ cups (430ml) water

¾ teaspoon fine sea salt, plus more as needed

VEGETABLES

1 cup / 150g green peas, fresh or frozen

1 pound / 450g (1 bunch) asparagus

FOR SERVING

½ cup / 60g raw, unsalted pumpkin seeds

1 bunch (about 12) radishes

Lemon-Mint Date Sauce, for serving (recipe follows)

Flaky sea salt

(recipe continues)

LEMON-MINT DATE SAUCE

MAKES ABOUT 1 CUP / 250ML

Zest and juice of 2 lemons

1 cup / 20g fresh mint leaves

3 to 4 soft pitted dates

¼ cup / 60ml cold-pressed olive oil

Pinch of fine sea salt

1 Using a food processor or immersion blender, purée the lemon zest and juice, mint, and dates until uniform in texture.

2 With the motor running, add the oil, and then thin the sauce with a little water until you get a consistency that you can drizzle. Season with the salt. Store leftovers in an airtight jar in the fridge for up to 4 days.

ROLLOVER Cook ⅓ cup / 55g extra quinoa for the Quinoa Corn Muffins (page 203).

GRILLED CAESAR SALAD

with Chickpea Croutons

As your friend, I am telling you that grilling lettuce may change your life forever. And at the very least it'll revolutionize your salad. Romaine is a hearty beast that stands up to the grill's high heat, while its structure can hold its shape during cooking. This technique brings crazy flavor to a rather bland leaf, and the Chickpea Croutons and Tahini Caesar Dressing take this dish to a place you've only dreamed of.

2 heads of romaine lettuce

Coconut oil, for rubbing

Fine sea salt

Tahini Caesar Dressing
(recipe follows)

Chickpea Croutons
(recipe follows)

SERVES 2 AS A MAIN, 4 AS A SIDE ————————————————————

1 Remove the looser outer leaves from the romaine heads (and save them for another salad) so all that remains are the tighter, inner leaves. Cut off the top quarter of each head (and save the tops for another salad). Slice the head in half lengthwise. Rub both the outsides and cut sides with a little coconut oil and sprinkle with a couple of pinches of sea salt.

2 Preheat a grill on high (a grill pan also works). When it is very hot, place the lettuce halves on the grill, cut-sides down, and cook until charred and grill marks appear, 3 to 4 minutes. Flip and cook for 2 to 3 minutes more.

3 To serve, place a lettuce half on each plate and let guests dress and garnish the salads themselves. (The croutons will soften quite quickly once in contact with the dressing, so it's best if diners add their own dressing.)

ROLLOVER Use the outer leaves and tops of the romaine lettuce in the Ginger-Pickled Carrot Lentil Salad with Spiced Prunes and Dukkah (page 85).

(recipe continues)

½ cup / 125ml tahini

1 garlic clove

½ teaspoon freshly ground black pepper

1 tablespoon cold-pressed olive oil

Zest of 1 lemon

1 tablespoon freshly squeezed lemon juice

2 teaspoons Dijon mustard

2 teaspoons gluten-free tamari

½ cup / 125ml water

Fine sea salt

TAHINI CAESAR DRESSING

MAKES ½ CUP / 125ML

In a blender, combine all the ingredients and blend on high until smooth, adding more water as necessary, up to 1 cup / 250ml total. Season with salt. Store leftover dressing in an airtight jar in the fridge for up to 1 week.

3 cups / 450g (2 15-oz. cans) cooked chickpeas, drained and rinsed

3 tablespoons coconut oil

1 teaspoon fine sea salt

1 teaspoon freshly ground black pepper

1 teaspoon garlic powder

CHICKPEA CROUTONS

MAKES 3 CUPS / 750ML

1 Preheat the oven to 400°F / 200°C.

2 Spread the chickpeas out on a clean kitchen towel and rub them dry, discarding any loose skins. Pour the chickpeas into a medium bowl and toss with the coconut oil, salt, pepper, and garlic powder.

3 Transfer the chickpeas to a rimmed baking sheet lined with parchment paper, and roast, stirring occasionally, until golden and crisp, 25 to 35 minutes.

4 Remove the baking sheet from the oven. Let the chickpeas cool, and serve them at room temperature. They will crisp up quite a bit once they've cooled, so don't worry if they are still a little soft when you take them out of the oven. Store the chickpeas in an airtight glass container at room temperature for up to 1 week.

COCONUT-QUINOA COLESLAW
with Minty Tahini Dressing

My friend Henriette is one of the most talented (and humble!) cooks that I know. We worked together at an organic vegetarian restaurant for years, and I learned so much from her, including how to think outside of the box and try new combinations of foods, even if they seemed unusual. One day she was making a cabbage salad and folded in toasted coconut. I looked over at what she was doing and raised an eyebrow . . . you can't mess with coleslaw! But it worked. Ever since then, I love tossing a little coconut into my cabbage salads. It adds sweet, nutty notes, and its richness is the perfect balance for the lightness of the cabbage. My version includes quinoa for a meal-like salad, but this is optional. The smooth and creamy Minty Tahini Dressing is ridiculously yummy on much more than this salad alone, so pour it onto everything you make—especially if it seems weird!

SERVES 6 AS A MAIN, 8 AS A SIDE

1 Make the quinoa: Rinse the quinoa well. In a small saucepan, combine the quinoa, water, and salt. Bring to a boil, reduce the heat to low, and cook, covered, until all the water has been absorbed and the quinoa grains are tender, about 20 minutes. Fluff with a fork.

2 Meanwhile, make the dressing: In a blender, combine the tahini, lime juice, olive oil, maple syrup, water, salt, and mint leaves; blend on high until smooth and creamy. Season with more salt as needed. Set aside.

3 In a large bowl, combine the cabbages, kale, carrots, and bell pepper.

QUINOA

½ cup / 85g quinoa, soaked if possible

Scant 1 cup / 250ml water

¼ teaspoon fine sea salt

MINTY TAHINI DRESSING

½ cup / 125ml tahini

¼ cup / 60ml freshly squeezed lime juice

2 tablespoons cold-pressed olive oil

1 tablespoon pure maple syrup

¾ cup / 185ml water

Pinch of sea salt, plus more as needed

1 packed cup / 25g fresh mint leaves

(recipe continues)

VEGETABLES

2 packed cups / 130g
shredded red cabbage

2 packed cups / 130g
shredded green cabbage

2 packed cups / 120g
shredded kale

3 medium carrots, julienned

1 red bell pepper (stem,
seeds, and ribs removed),
julienned

¼ cup / 60ml freshly
squeezed lemon juice

1 tablespoon cold-pressed
olive oil

¼ teaspoon fine sea salt

1 cup / 100g unsweetened
desiccated coconut

4 In a small bowl, whisk the lemon juice, olive oil, and salt together and pour over the vegetables. Toss well and lightly massage the liquid into the kale and cabbage, then let marinate for 5 to 10 minutes.

5 Preheat a dry skillet over medium heat. When hot, toast the coconut, stirring often, until golden brown and fragrant, 2 to 3 minutes. Immediately remove the pan from the heat and set it aside.

6 Finish the salad: Add the quinoa and coconut to the vegetable bowl. Toss well to combine. When ready to serve, dish out portions and allow guests to pour the dressing on their salads.

ROLLOVER **Make a double batch of the dressing for the Snappy Spring Salad (page 57).**

SPROUTED MUNG BEAN

and Mango Avocado Cups

(V) (GF) (R) (GrF)

For as long as I can remember, one of my mother's favorite snacks has been half an avocado scooped out and dressed with a little salt and lemon. When I was a kid the mere idea of this made me ill, but now the only thing I think could be better is the *entire* avocado. Very much inspired by my mom, this salad is a celebration of the steps I've taken toward a healthier life. Crunchy mung bean sprouts, juicy sweet mango, and lime combine to make a tropical-tasting treat that you could eat any time of the day—it actually makes a fantastic breakfast! This recipe calls for two large avocados to serve four people, but if you're anything like me, you'll go for a whole one too.

SERVES 2 AS A MAIN, 4 AS A SIDE ———————————————

1 Make the dressing: In a small bowl, whisk together the lime juice, olive oil, and salt.

2 Prepare the salad: Peel and cut the mango into bite-size pieces. In a large bowl, combine the mango with the bean sprouts, cilantro, shallot, and pepper flakes. Pour the dressing over top and toss to coat. Season with salt.

3 Slice the avocados in half and remove the pits and a small portion of the flesh to create a space in each half for the filling.

4 Fold the extra avocado flesh into the salad, then fill each avocado with plenty of salad, letting it spill over the sides. Serve immediately.

ROLLOVER Make extra sprouted mung bean salad and serve it over cooked brown rice for a complete lunch the next day.

DRESSING

2 tablespoons freshly squeezed lime juice

1 tablespoon cold-pressed olive oil

2 pinches of flaky sea salt

SALAD

1 large ripe mango

3 cups / 180g mung bean sprouts (see Basic Sprouts, page 23)

½ packed cup / 20g chopped fresh cilantro leaves and tender stems

1 shallot or ¼ red onion, minced

A few pinches of crushed red pepper flakes

Fine sea salt

2 large ripe avocados

TERRIFIC TARRAGON
GREEN BEAN SALAD

½ cup / 85g raw, unsalted pecans

1 pound / 400g fresh green beans

6 ounces / 175g green peas, fresh or frozen

1 small red onion or a couple of shallots, minced

⅓ cup / 15g chopped fresh tarragon leaves

Maple-Mustard Dressing (recipe follows)

5 ounces / 150g feta cheese (preferably goat or sheep), crumbled

Fine sea salt

1 teaspoon freshly ground black pepper

ROLLOVER If you have any extra tarragon, use it to replace the cilantro in the Deep Detox Cilantro, Spinach, and Sweet Potato Soup (page 43).

This is one juicy jewel box of a salad! Sweet green peas, tender green beans, shallots, feta, and pecans shine bright and beautifully together. Enjoy this in late spring and summer when beans and peas are fresh and in season. If you're not familiar with tarragon, it tastes like a combination of licorice and basil with a pleasant lemony aftertaste. It also goes very well with other green foods, such as asparagus and artichokes, and it's especially delicious when combined with a strong mustard. If you want to make this ahead of time for a picnic or a potluck, leave the dressing, cheese, and nuts out until right before serving.

SERVES 2 AS A MAIN, 4 AS A SIDE ────────────────

1 Start the salad: Preheat the oven to 350°F / 180°C. Place the pecans on a rimmed baking sheet and toast until fragrant, 5 to 7 minutes. Remove from the oven and set aside.

2 Cook the vegetables: Wash and trim the green beans. In a large pot fitted with a steamer basket, bring a small amount of water to a boil. Add the green beans and steam until crisp-tender, 4 to 5 minutes, being careful not to overcook. Remove the beans from the steamer basket and rinse them under cold water to halt the cooking process.

3 Return the steamer basket to the pot and add the peas to the basket. Steam the peas until bright green and sweet, 1 to 2 minutes. Drain and rinse them under cold water to halt the cooking process.

4 Finish the salad: Place the green beans and peas in a large bowl with the red onion and tarragon. Pour the dressing over top, toss to coat, and sprinkle with the feta and pecans. Season with sea salt and the freshly ground black pepper.

MAPLE-MUSTARD DRESSING

MAKES A LITTLE MORE THAN ¼ CUP / (55ML)

In a small bowl, whisk together the olive oil, maple syrup, mustard, and vinegar. Season with salt and pepper. The dressing will keep, refrigerated in an airtight container, for up to 1 week.

3 tablespoons cold-pressed olive oil

1½ teaspoons pure maple syrup

1 tablespoon Dijon mustard

1 tablespoon apple cider vinegar

Pinch of fine sea salt

Freshly ground black pepper

BALSAMIC-ROASTED PLUMS

with Spinach and Goat Cheese

SALAD

4 medium plums (choose ones that are a little firmer than ripe)

1 teaspoon coconut oil or ghee, melted

1 tablespoon balsamic vinegar

½ teaspoon freshly ground black pepper, plus more for serving

4 cups / 100g baby spinach

3½ ounces / 100g soft goat cheese

BALSAMIC DRESSING

2 tablespoons cold-pressed olive oil

1½ teaspoons balsamic vinegar

1 teaspoon Dijon mustard

1 shallot, minced

Pinch of fine sea salt, plus more for serving

This is a very simple and just plain yummy salad. Roasting the plums caramelizes and deepens the flavor of their sugars, while the balsamic vinegar adds a contrasting sour note. The salad would also be lovely topped with something crunchy, such as toasted almonds or walnuts. To make this dish even more substantial, add some cooked lentils and serve it with your favorite gluten-free bread or some crusty whole-grain sourdough.

SERVES 2 AS A MAIN, 4 AS A SIDE

1 Prepare the salad: Preheat the oven to 350°F / 180°C.

2 Pit the plums and slice them into eighths. On a rimmed baking sheet lined with parchment paper, toss the plum slices with the melted coconut oil, balsamic vinegar, and black pepper. Roast, turning once, until the plums are soft and caramelized, 15 to 20 minutes. Let cool.

3 Meanwhile, wash the spinach and spin it dry. Transfer to a large bowl.

4 Make the dressing: In a small bowl, whisk together the olive oil, vinegar, mustard, shallot, and salt. Pour the dressing over the spinach and toss to coat.

5 Finish the salad: Scatter the plums over the dressed spinach and crumble the goat cheese on top. Season with salt and pepper.

ROLLOVER Roast extra plums to use in the Copycat Couscous with Clementines (page 175) instead of the clementines.

EMERALD CITY SALAD

This is more of an idea than a recipe, and one that came to me while I was eating at a friend's place. We both love avocados, and before putting them in the salad she was serving, my friend cut them into rings. Rings! What a simple change to make, and what a beautiful impact it had—it was like eating a completely different vegetable. Inspired by this, I created a green-on-green salad with cucumber ribbons, lime juice, mint, and red pepper flakes for a result that sparkles and shimmers. You'll be off to see the Wizard with this easy, warm-weather dish!

SERVES 2 AS A MAIN, 4 AS A SIDE ──────────────────

2 ripe avocados

½ cup / 10g fresh mint leaves

1 large cucumber, preferably an English cucumber

Juice of 1 lime

1 tablespoon cold-pressed olive oil

½ teaspoon crushed red pepper flakes

Flaky sea salt

1 Slice the avocados crosswise and around the pit into ¼-inch / 0.5cm rings. Peel the skin off and place the flesh on a large serving platter. Stack the mint leaves, roll them into a cigar shape, and slice them crosswise to create ribbons.

2 Using a mandoline slicer, cut the cucumber (including the skin) lengthwise into long ribbons. Layer the cucumber with the avocado rings on the platter.

3 Pour the lime juice evenly over top, drizzle with the olive oil, and sprinkle with the pepper flakes, mint, and sea salt. Serve immediately.

ROLLOVER Save any leftover salad for the Rainbow Hummus Bowl (page 74).

RAINBOW HUMMUS BOWL

⅓ cup / 75ml hummus of your choice

Fresh greens (such as spinach, arugula, and romaine)

Handful of cooked beans or lentils

Handful of sprouts

Mix of chopped veggies (such as steamed green beans; roasted beets; raw bell pepper, carrots, and/or avocado; and olives)

FOR SERVING

Cold-pressed olive oil

Freshly squeezed lemon juice

Flaky sea salt

When I was in Los Angeles, I visited a brand-new raw-food restaurant that offered a falafel salad bowl—basically my dream come true on any menu. When the dish arrived, the vegetables themselves were lightly dressed, and the main attraction—a rich and delicious hummus—was generously smeared around the inside of the bowl so that each bite I took was adorned with it. Brilliant! I re-created it as soon as I got home, choosing an abundance of seasonal veggies prepared in a variety of ways, and using the hummus I had in the fridge at the time. This works any time of the year with any kind of hummus and is *the* perfect clean-out-the-fridge meal. Try it with one of the hummus recipes on pages 187–89.

SERVES 1 AS A MAIN

1 Smear the hummus around the inside of a single-serve salad bowl.

2 Add the greens, beans, sprouts, and veggies, and toss. Drizzle with olive oil and lemon juice and season with salt. Toss to coat.

ROLLOVER Sprout extra lentils to make the Sprouted Lentil Chili (page 138).

TOMATOES

with Basil and Sunflower Meta Feta

SUNFLOWER META FETA

3 cups / 420g raw, unsalted, shelled sunflower seeds, soaked for at least 2 hours, preferably overnight, drained and rinsed

1 teaspoon fine sea salt

1 large garlic clove

¼ cup / 60ml freshly squeezed lemon juice

⅓ cup / 80ml water

CAPER DRESSING

3 tablespoons cold-pressed olive oil

1½ teaspoons apple cider vinegar

1 tablespoon pure maple syrup

2 pinches of fine sea salt, plus more as needed

½ garlic clove, finely minced

2 tablespoons capers, rinsed

4 medium tomatoes, in season if possible

Flaky sea salt

Freshly ground black pepper

Handful of fresh basil leaves

Tomatoes, basil, and cheese is a well-loved, classic combination. But my curious heart has always wanted to make a vegan version. Introducing, "meta feta": a spreadable sunflower seed "cheese" with tons of flavor and versatility, perfect for salads, sandwiches, and filling wraps.

This dish is delicious all year round, but because the main attraction is tomatoes you'll have the most delicious results in late summer, when they're at their peak of ripeness.

SERVES 2 AS A MAIN, 4 AS A SIDE ——————————————

1 Make the Meta Feta: Place the soaked and drained sunflower seeds, salt, garlic clove, and lemon juice in a food processor. Pulse a few times to break down the seeds. Turn the motor on and drizzle the water into the machine in a thin stream as the mixture is processed. Stop a few times to scrape down the bowl. You're aiming for the texture of a thick, chunky hummus; add just enough additional water (up to ½ cup / 125ml) to achieve that texture. Transfer the mixture to an airtight container and refrigerate it for at least 30 minutes before using. This will keep in an airtight container in the refrigerator for up to 4 days.

2 Meanwhile, prepare the Caper Dressing: Whisk together the olive oil, vinegar, maple syrup, salt, garlic, and capers. Taste and adjust the seasonings, if necessary.

3 To serve, spread ½ cup / 125g of the Meta Feta on a large platter or serving dish. Slice the tomatoes and lay them across the top. Season the salad with salt and pepper, sprinkle with the basil leaves, and drizzle the Caper Dressing over the top.

ROLLOVER Use the extra Meta Feta from this recipe to make the Eggplant Cannelloni with Sunflower Feta and Toasted Garlic Tomato Sauce (page 114).

CELERY LEAF SALAD
with Balsamic Roasted Eggplant

Isn't it strange how we become accustomed to eating some parts of fruits and vegetables but not others? Celery leaves are the perfect example of this—we are so used to eating the stalk and tossing the rest away, but the leaves are supremely delicious. Waste not, want not! With an intense freshness and a pleasing bitterness, they pair with earthy flavors like eggplant and walnuts. This salad is a hearty dish and makes a wonderful lunch or light dinner.

SERVES 2 AS A MAIN, 4 AS A SIDE

1 Preheat the oven to 400°F / 200°C.

2 Whisk together the vinegar, mustard, pepper flakes, and salt in a large bowl.

3 Slice the unpeeled eggplant into rounds approximately ½ inch / 1.3cm thick. Add to the bowl with the dressing and toss well to coat. Let marinate for 5 minutes. Place the eggplant slices on a rimmed baking sheet lined with parchment paper and spoon some of the extra marinade on top, reserving the rest for the last step. Roast for 10 minutes, then flip and roast on the other side until tender, 5 to 10 minutes more. Remove from the oven, crumble the goat cheese over top, and broil until golden, 2 to 3 minutes.

4 Lower the oven temperature to 325°F / 160°C. Place the walnuts on another rimmed baking sheet and toast until fragrant, about 7 to 10 minutes, watching them carefully so they do not burn. Remove the walnuts from the oven and roughly chop.

5 Wash and dry the celery leaves and place them in a medium bowl. Whisk the olive oil in with the remaining marinade. Pour over the celery leaves and toss to coat. Divide the celery leaves among plates, top with a few slices of eggplant, and sprinkle the walnuts over top.

¼ cup / 60ml balsamic vinegar

1 tablespoon Dijon mustard

½ teaspoon crushed red pepper flakes

¼ teaspoon fine sea salt

1 eggplant

2½ ounces / 75g soft goat cheese

⅓ cup / 40g raw, unsalted walnuts

3 packed cups / 60g celery leaves

1 tablespoon cold-pressed olive oil

SHINING SUMMER GRILLED ZUCCHINI AND CORN

with Basil

2 ears of corn

2 teaspoons coconut oil

2 zucchini

Flaky sea salt

Lemon Garlic Dressing
(page 54)

¼ cup / 30g pumpkin seeds

9 ounces / 250g cherry
tomatoes, whole or halved

Handful of fresh basil leaves

Crushed red pepper flakes

ROLLOVER Grill 4 extra ears
of corn and use them in the
Cashew Corn Chowder with
Chipotle Oil (page 38). Double
up the Lemon Garlic Dressing
for the Roasted Sweet Potato
and Butter Beans on Massaged
Kale (page 54).

This is pure summer on a plate and the perfect example of how things that grow together taste amazing together! Although you can purchase these ingredients all year round, I highly recommend making this when the corn, zucchini, tomatoes, and basil are fresh and bountiful and your grill is enjoying a healthy workout. To change things up, try this salad with cilantro or mint, use roasted hazelnuts or almonds, and put it all on a bed of black beans for a heartier dish.

SERVES 2 AS A MAIN, 4 AS A SIDE ——————————————

1 Heat the grill to high. Husk the ears of corn and rub them with a little of the coconut oil. Place them on the grill and cook, turning every few minutes, until tender and bright yellow. Remove from the grill and let them cool. Cut off the corn kernels by standing each ear on its end in a shallow bowl and slicing downward.

2 Slice the zucchini lengthwise into ¼-inch- / 0.5cm-thick pieces (not too thin or they will fall apart on the grill). Rub both sides of each slice with a little coconut oil and place on the grill. Cook, flipping once, until both sides are tender and lightly charred. Remove the zucchini from the grill and place in the bowl with the corn. Season with the flaky sea salt.

3 Pour half of the dressing over the corn and zucchini. Toss gently to coat and let the vegetables marinate for 5 minutes.

4 Preheat a small dry skillet over medium heat. When hot, toast the pumpkin seeds, tossing often, until fragrant, 3 to 5 minutes. Immediately remove the pan from the heat and set it aside.

5 Place the zucchini and corn on a large serving platter. Add the tomatoes and basil, pour the remaining dressing over top, and sprinkle with the pumpkin seeds and pepper flakes. Serve immediately.

ARUGULA AND FIG SALAD
with Toasted Walnut Sauce

2½ ounces / 75g arugula

3 large ripe figs

1 small red onion or shallot

Toasted Walnut Sauce, for serving (recipe follows)

Figs have the undeniable ability to turn any dish into a special one. The fact that they are only around for a few weeks a year makes me appreciate their uniqueness even more. This salad is an exceptional way to enjoy figs' fleeting moment, especially when paired with Toasted Walnut Sauce. The sauce's roasted-nut flavor and creamy texture will blow your mind! Here it combines perfectly with the mellow sweetness of figs, but try it on pasta and roasted veggies too.

SERVES 2 AS A MAIN, 4 AS A SIDE

1 Wash and dry the arugula.

2 Slice the figs into quarters. Slice the onions into thin rounds.

3 Divide all of the ingredients among plates. Drizzle with Toasted Walnut Sauce.

ROLLOVER Make extra Toasted Walnut Sauce for the Charred Cabbage with Apples and Toasted Walnut Sauce (page 179) or the Wild Rice, Roasted Carrot, and Pomegranate Bold Bowl (page 147).

(recipe continues)

V GF GrF

1 cup / 125g raw, unsalted walnuts

1 garlic clove

2 tablespoons cold-pressed olive oil

4 teaspoons apple cider vinegar

2 teaspoons pure maple syrup or raw honey

2 generous pinches of fine sea salt, plus more as needed

TOASTED WALNUT SAUCE

MAKES APPROXIMATELY 1 CUP / 270ML

1 Preheat the oven to 350°F / 180°C.

2 Spread the walnuts in a single layer on a rimmed baking sheet. Toast until they are golden and fragrant, 7 to 10 minutes, watching them carefully so they do not burn. Remove from the oven and let cool slightly.

3 Add the toasted walnuts, garlic, olive oil, apple cider vinegar, and maple syrup to a blender. Blend on high, adding 1 cup / 250ml of water to thin the dressing as needed—you are looking for the consistency of melted ice cream. Season with salt. Store in an airtight glass container in the fridge for up to 5 days.

GINGER-PICKLED CARROT LENTIL SALAD

with Spiced Prunes and Dukkah

There is a wonderful balance of flavors going on here: the acidity of the carrots, the sweetness of the prunes, and the deep spices from the dressing. You can make a couple of the elements ahead of time, and in fact, I recommend doing so. The carrots do not need a full twenty-four hours to pickle, but if you desire the full effect, it's the only way to go! The lentils can be cooked in advance and stored in the fridge so that all you have to do is toss everything together right before you serve. Most green lettuces will work here, but the softer, creamier Boston, butter, and Bibb lettuces are my favorites.

SERVES 4 AS A MAIN, 6 AS A SIDE

1 In small pot, cover the lentils with about 3 cups / 750ml of water and bring to a boil over high heat. Reduce the heat to low and simmer, covered, until tender but not mushy, 10 to 20 minutes, depending on whether or not you soaked them. Add the salt about 5 minutes before the lentils are done. Drain and lightly rinse the cooked lentils.

2 Make the dressing: Whisk together the olive oil, lemon juice, cumin, cinnamon, coriander, paprika, and salt. Pour half of the dressing over the lentils while they are still warm, and fold to coat.

3 Wash and dry the lettuce well. Separate the leaves and place in a large bowl or on a platter. Roughly chop the mint. Scatter the lentils over the lettuce, top with the pickled carrots, prunes, and Dukkah, and drizzle the remaining dressing over the top. Season with flaky salt. Sprinkle the salad with the mint leaves and serve.

1 cup / 200g green lentils, soaked for 8 hours or overnight if possible

½ teaspoon fine sea salt

DRESSING

3 tablespoons cold-pressed olive oil

¼ cup / 60ml freshly squeezed lemon juice

2 teaspoons ground cumin

1 teaspoon ground cinnamon

¼ teaspoon ground coriander

¼ teaspoon smoked hot paprika (ground chipotle would also work)

2 pinches of fine sea salt, plus more as needed

1 small head tender lettuce

¼ packed cup / 5g fresh mint leaves

Ginger-Pickled Carrots (recipe follows)

½ cup / 85g pitted prunes, chopped

3 tablespoons Dukkah (page 26)

Flaky sea salt

(recipe continues)

GINGER-PICKLED CARROTS

MAKES ONE 1-QUART / 1-LITER JAR

4 or 5 medium carrots

1 cup / 250ml apple cider vinegar

1 cup / 250ml water, plus more as needed

1 tablespoon pure maple syrup

1½ teaspoons fine sea salt

Small knob of fresh ginger (about 3½ ounces / 10g), peeled and sliced

1 Scrub the carrots well. Using a vegetable peeler, slice the carrots lengthwise into long, thin ribbons. Place the ribbons in a 1-quart / 1-liter glass container.

2 In a measuring cup, combine the vinegar, water, maple syrup, salt, and ginger, and stir to dissolve the salt. Pour the brine over the carrots and add more water as needed to cover them completely. Seal the container and place the carrots in the fridge for at least 30 minutes, ideally 24 hours, before using. The carrots will keep in the refrigerator for up to 3 weeks.

ROLLOVER Use the Ginger-Pickled Carrots in the Grilled Eggplant and Mushrooms with Saucy Almond Butter Noodles (page 133).

CRAVEABLE CREAMY BRUSSELS SPROUT SLAW

with Apple and Toasted Almonds

SLAW

⅓ cup / 50g raw almonds

1 packed cup / 30g fresh flat-leaf parsley leaves and stems

½ pound / 250g Brussels sprouts

1 apple

2 teaspoons freshly squeezed lemon juice

CREAMY MAPLE VINAIGRETTE

2 tablespoons cold-pressed olive oil

4 teaspoons Dijon mustard

4 teaspoons apple cider vinegar

2 teaspoons pure maple syrup

¼ cup / 65g plain yogurt (preferably goat or sheep; optional)

2 pinches of fine sea salt

2 pinches of freshly ground black pepper, plus more as needed

If any of you out there think that Brussels sprouts are absolutely uncraveable, this salad is here to show you otherwise! Simple, fresh, and quite addictive, this dish is wonderful in the cooler months when Brussels and apples are at their peak.

The apple adds sweetness, the toasted almonds bring satisfying crunch and nuttiness, and the parsley lends major brightness. Hazelnuts would be another delicious nut option here.

SERVES 2 AS A MAIN, 4 AS A SIDE

1 Prepare the slaw: Preheat the oven to 300°F / 150°C. Spread the almonds on a rimmed baking sheet in a single layer and roast until fragrant and slightly darker in color, 20 to 25 minutes. (A good way to check is to bite one in half and check the color in the center—it should be golden.) Remove from the oven and let cool completely. Roughly chop the almonds and the parsley leaves, finely mincing the stems.

2 While the almonds are roasting, wash and trim the Brussels sprouts, removing any damaged outer leaves. Slice them as thinly as possible using a knife or a food processor with the shredding attachment. Place in a large bowl.

3 Core and slice the apple into thin sections. In a small bowl, immediately toss the apple sections with the lemon juice to prevent browning.

4 Make the dressing: Whisk together the olive oil, mustard, apple cider vinegar, maple syrup, yogurt, salt, and pepper.

5 Add the apples, almonds, and parsley to the shredded Brussels, pour the dressing over top, add a generous amount of black pepper, and fold to combine.

ROLLOVER Roast double the almonds and use them for Twinkle, Twinkle, Jeweled Rice (page 176).

ROLLOVER Double the amount of cooked quinoa to use in the
Quinoa and Black Beans with Radish Cilantro Salsa (page 106).

LEMONY RAW BEET AND QUINOA SALAD

with Dill and Olives

Raw beets are one of my favorite foods. They are crisp yet tender, earthy and sweet. If you are one of the many people who have only tried cooked beets, be prepared to fall in love. The secret to the tastiest raw beets is to cut them very thinly. A mandoline slicer is the best tool to create paper-thin slivers, but if you are confident with your knife skills, you can go the old-fashioned route. This salad is vegan, but if you are serving people who don't mind dairy, feta cheese is really lovely folded in.

SERVES 4 AS A MAIN, 6 AS A SIDE

1 Rinse the quinoa well. In a small saucepan, combine the quinoa, water, and salt. Bring to a boil, reduce the heat to low, and cook, covered, until all the water has been absorbed and the grains are tender, about 20 minutes. Fluff with a fork.

2 While the quinoa is cooking, peel the beets and thinly slice them with a mandoline. In a medium bowl, toss the beet slices with the freshly squeezed lemon juice. Set aside.

3 Pour half of the dressing and sprinkle the lemon zest over the cooked quinoa while it is still warm; toss to coat.

4 Preheat a small dry skillet over medium heat. When hot, toast the pistachios, stirring often, until fragrant, about 5 minutes. Immediately remove the pan from the heat, let the nuts cool, and then roughly chop them.

5 Transfer the quinoa to a large bowl or serving platter. Add the sliced shallot and dill to the quinoa; fold to combine. Tuck the beet slices into the quinoa (if you toss them in, the quinoa will turn pink!), then add the olives and chopped pistachios. Drizzle the remaining dressing over the salad and season with salt.

1 cup / 190g quinoa, soaked if possible

1¾ cups / 415ml water

¾ teaspoon fine sea salt

1 medium beet

1 tablespoon freshly squeezed lemon juice

Lemon Garlic Dressing (page 54)

Zest of 1 lemon

⅓ cup / 50g raw, unsalted pistachios

1 shallot, sliced

1 packed cup / 55g chopped fresh dill

1 cup / 130g mixed green olives, with pits

nourishing
MAINS

PREVIOUS PAGE, from left to right: Massaged Kale, Feta, and Pecans, page 96 / Mediterranean
Broccoli and Chickpeas, page 97 / Spicy Cabbage and Black Beans, page 97

STUFFED SWEET POTATOES, 3 WAYS

If you read the *My New Roots* blog, you'll know just how obsessed I am with sweet potatoes. I love their versatility, incredible taste, and astounding nutritional profile. They are very easy to serve roasted whole, sliced open, and stuffed with whatever you're in the mood for. I get a lot of pleasure out of assemble-it-yourself food. Having a whole buffet of tasty things to mix and match at will makes me totally giddy. You can make one, two, or all three of these toppings for a buffet to suit any tastes, but I usually stick to just one on a weeknight. One stuffed potato makes a complete and satisfying lunch, dinner, or even breakfast. Each of the toppings included here makes enough for about four medium sweet potatoes with extras—because you'll always want extra!

The skin of sweet potatoes is the most nutritious part of the vegetable, so try to find organic sweet potatoes if you can.

WHOLE ROASTED SWEET POTATOES

SERVES 4

4 medium sweet potatoes

Cold-pressed olive oil, melted butter, or ghee, for drizzling

Filling of your choice (pages 96 and 97)

1 Preheat the oven to 450°F / 230°C.

2 Scrub the sweet potatoes well, pierce them with a fork in a few places, and set them on a rimmed baking sheet. Bake for 25 to 30 minutes, depending on the size of the potatoes. The potatoes are cooked when you can easily insert a sharp knife into the center. Remove from the oven and slice each one lengthwise, making sure not to cut them into two pieces. Drizzle with a little olive oil.

3 Serve the potatoes with one or more of the suggested fillings that follow. Undressed roasted sweet potatoes will keep in the fridge for up to 3 days. Reheat in a 400°F / 200°C oven for 10 minutes.

(recipe continues)

MASSAGED KALE, FETA, AND PECANS FILLING

½ cup / 50g raw, unsalted pecans

3 cups / 90g shredded curly kale

Juice of ½ lemon

2 teaspoons cold-pressed olive oil

2 pinches of fine sea salt, plus more as needed

½ cup / 50g crumbled feta

SERVES 4 ————————————————————————

1 Preheat the oven to 300°F / 150°C. Spread the pecans on a rimmed baking sheet in a single layer and roast them until fragrant and slightly darker in color, 12 to 15 minutes. (A good way to check for doneness is to bite one in half and check the color in the center—it should be golden.) Remove from the oven and let cool completely. Roughly chop the pecans.

2 In a large bowl, combine the shredded kale, lemon juice, olive oil, and salt. Using your hands, rub and squeeze the kale together as if you are giving it a massage, until the kale leaves are dark green and tender, about 2 minutes. Add the feta and pecans, toss everything to combine, and season with salt.

MEDITERRANEAN BROCCOLI AND CHICKPEAS FILLING

SERVES 4 ——————————————

In a large bowl, whisk together the lemon zest and juice, olive oil, ½ teaspoon salt, and maple syrup. Add the broccoli, chickpeas, olives, and pine nuts. Toss to combine and season with salt.

Zest of 1 lemon

Juice of ½ lemon

1 tablespoon cold-pressed olive oil

½ teaspoon fine sea salt, plus more as needed

1 teaspoon pure maple syrup or raw honey

2 cups / 160g diced broccoli, both tops and stems

1½ cups / 225g (1 15-oz. can) chickpeas, drained and rinsed

¼ cup / 40g pitted olives (kalamata is good choice)

¼ cup / 25g pine nuts

SPICY CABBAGE AND BLACK BEANS FILLING

SERVES 4 ——————————————

In a large bowl, combine the shredded cabbage, black beans, lime juice, olive oil, salt, cilantro, spring onions, and red chile.

2 cups / 150g shredded red cabbage

1½ cups / 250g (1 15-oz. can) black beans, drained and rinsed

Juice of 1 lime

1 tablespoon cold-pressed olive oil

A few pinches of fine sea salt

½ cup / 15g chopped fresh cilantro leaves

2 spring onions, white and green parts, sliced

1 small red chile (seeds removed), sliced (serrano is a good choice)

FANTASTIC FALAFEL WAFFLES

2 cups / 400g dried chickpeas

3 tablespoons freshly squeezed lemon juice or apple cider vinegar

1 heaping cup / 115g gluten-free rolled oats

2 garlic cloves

½ packed cup / 15g chopped fresh flat-leaf parsley

½ packed cup / 20g chopped fresh cilantro leaves and tender stems

1½ teaspoons ground cumin

1½ teaspoons ground cinnamon

2 teaspoons ground coriander

1½ teaspoons fine sea salt

1 teaspoon freshly ground black pepper

Zest of 1 lemon

Coconut oil, for greasing the waffle iron

2 tablespoons raw, unsalted sesame seeds

Spicy Lime Slaw (recipe follows)

Harissa Tahini Sauce (recipe follows)

Finely sliced red onion

Avocado slices

2 handfuls of your favorite sprouts

Crushed red pepper flakes

Falafels sit at the top of my list for most attempts at a healthy makeover and at the bottom of my list for successful homemade meals. Why are they so darn delicious at a restaurant and so darn underwhelming at home? The secret, and most important aspect of awesome falafels, is to not cook your chickpeas. Nope. Use raw chickpeas and soak them for twenty-four hours (so make sure to start this recipe a day ahead of time).

MAKES 10 TO 12 WAFFLES

1 In a large bowl, cover the chickpeas with plenty of water and 2 tablespoons of the lemon juice. Let soak for 24 hours, then drain and rinse them very well. Set aside.

2 In a food processor, pulse the oats until a roughly textured flour forms. Transfer the oat flour to a bowl and set aside. Without cleaning the food processor, add the garlic and pulse to mince. Add the chickpeas, chopped herbs, spices, lemon zest, and the remaining tablespoon of lemon juice. Pulse until the chickpeas are very finely minced but not pasty. Transfer the contents to a large mixing bowl.

3 Add the oat flour to the chickpea mixture and mix well, then add ¼ cup / 60ml water a spoonful at a time, stirring in between additions, until the dough holds together well when pressed.

4 Heat a waffle iron to medium-high and preheat the oven to 200°F / 95°C. Brush the iron with a little coconut oil. Divide the falafel dough into 10 to 12 equal portions, gently packing each portion so that it holds together well, especially around the edges. Flatten out a portion and press it into the hot waffle iron with the back of a spatula, then lower the lid and cook the falafel until it is golden brown and crisp, anywhere from 5 to 10 minutes, depending on your iron. Transfer the falafel from the waffle iron to a parchment-lined rimmed baking sheet and keep it in the warm oven until ready to serve. Repeat with the remaining portions, brushing the iron with more coconut oil, if necessary.

5 While the waffles are cooking, heat a dry skillet over medium heat. Add the sesame seeds and toast, stirring often, until fragrant and just beginning to pop, 3 to 4 minutes. Remove from heat.

6 Serve the hot falafel waffles with the Spicy Lime Slaw, Harissa Tahini Sauce, toasted sesame seeds, red onion, avocado, sprouts, pepper flakes, and anything else you fancy!

SPICY LIME SLAW

MAKES APPROXIMATELY 4 CUPS / 300G

In a large bowl, combine the cabbage, salt, and lime juice. Massage the cabbage for about a minute until it begins to wilt. Drizzle with the olive oil and maple syrup. Season with more salt, as desired, and fold in the herbs and chile. Store leftovers in an airtight container in the fridge for up to 2 days.

4 cups / 300g finely shredded red cabbage

½ teaspoon fine sea salt, plus more as needed

1½ teaspoons freshly squeezed lime juice

1 tablespoon cold-pressed olive oil

1 teaspoon pure maple syrup or raw honey, plus more as needed

Handful of chopped fresh flat-leaf parsley or fresh cilantro leaves and tender stems, or both

1 small red chile (seeds removed), sliced (serrano is a good choice)

HARISSA TAHINI SAUCE

MAKES ABOUT 1 CUP / 250ML

In a blender, combine the tahini, garlic, lemon juice, olive oil, harissa paste, maple syrup, and a pinch of salt. Blend on high until smooth and creamy, adding approximately ½ cup / 125ml of water to thin the sauce as desired. The sauce will keep in an airtight container in the fridge for up to 1 week.

⅓ cup / 80ml tahini

1 large garlic clove, finely minced

2 tablespoons freshly squeezed lemon juice

1 tablespoon cold-pressed olive oil

2 teaspoons gluten-free harissa paste (available at Middle Eastern grocery stores)

1 teaspoon pure maple syrup or raw honey

Fine sea salt

RUN WILD SUMMER ROLLS

Whether you're having friends over for dinner or you're just trying to impress yourself, these fresh and lively summer rolls will do the trick. Although there is a bit of prep involved, they aren't complicated, and once all the chopping is complete, they assemble really quickly. This recipe uses three different building blocks that you can make ahead or take from other recipes—the Radish Cilantro Salsa, the Spicy Lime Slaw, and the Almond Butter Sauce—but you can really use any number of fresh salads, noodles, veggies, and dipping sauces. The Spicy Tahini Ginger Sauce (page 104) is particularly good with these rolls. Let your imagination run wild and get rolling!

SERVES 2 AS A MAIN (4 ROLLS PER PERSON) ———————

1 Preheat a small dry skillet over medium heat. When hot, toast the sesame seeds, stirring frequently, until fragrant, 2 to 3 minutes. Remove the pan from the heat and set aside.

2 Fill a shallow dish a little larger than the rice paper wraps with room-temperature water. Place one wrap in the water until it becomes soft and pliable but not completely limp, about 1 minute.

3 Transfer the wrap to a clean work surface and place a little salsa, slaw, carrot, avocado, sprouts, a sprinkling of sesame seeds, and a few mint leaves in the center, plus a drizzle of sauce (avoid the temptation to overstuff with fillings).

4 Fold the top half of the wrap over the fillings. Then fold in both sides. Lastly, fold the bottom up to seal. If the rice paper breaks or it seems like the whole thing is going to fall apart (don't worry, it does sometimes), you can simply reinforce the roll by wrapping it in another sheet of soaked rice paper. Repeat steps 2 to 4 to make 7 more rolls. Serve immediately with the remaining sauce.

¼ cup / 40g raw, unsalted sesame seeds

8 rice paper wraps

Radish Cilantro Salsa (page 108)

Spicy Lime Slaw (page 99)

1 medium carrot, julienned

1 ripe avocado, sliced

1 cup / 50g sprouts

Handful of fresh mint leaves

Almond Butter Sauce (page 135)

ROLLOVER Make a double batch of the Radish Cilantro Salsa for the Quinoa and Black Beans with Radish Cilantro Salsa (page 106).

SURPRISING SUNFLOWER SEED RISOTTO

2½ cups / 350g raw, unsalted, shelled sunflower seeds

2 tablespoons fine sea salt, plus more as needed

1 tablespoon coconut oil or ghee

2 medium yellow onions, finely diced

5 garlic cloves, minced

2 cups / 500ml vegetable broth

1 pound / 450g (1 bunch) asparagus, stems removed, roughly chopped

1 cup / 150g shelled fresh green peas

FOR SERVING

Cold-pressed olive oil

Small handful of chopped fresh flat-leaf parsley

Flaky sea salt

Lemon wedges

To say that this recipe is *totally* surprising would be an understatement. Rice-less risotto made from sunflower seeds?! It may just be the wildest thing I've ever cooked—successfully, anyway. The sunflower seeds are tender and chewy, with just the slightest bit of toothiness—not unlike rice cooked al dente. It's remarkably simple to make with just a few common ingredients, truly delicious, and deeply satisfying. The seeds create a foundation you can build upon no matter what time of year it is, so feel free to make it with any seasonal vegetables. I chose to go the spring route with peas and asparagus, but this would be equally as lovely with sautéed mushrooms, roasted root vegetables, pumpkin, or squash.

SERVES 4 —————————————————————————

1 Soak the sunflower seeds overnight or all day with the sea salt in a large bowl of filtered water.

2 Drain and rinse the sunflower seeds. In a blender, add 1 cup / 135g of the soaked seeds and 1 cup / 250ml water and blend on high until smooth. Set aside.

3 In a large stockpot, melt the coconut oil over medium-high heat. Add the onions and a pinch of sea salt, stir to coat, and cook until translucent, 5 to 7 minutes. Add the garlic and cook for 2 minutes more. Add the remaining whole sunflower seeds and just enough of the broth to cover the seeds. Reduce the heat to low and simmer, covered, for 20 to 30 minutes. The seeds are done when they are al dente, tender with only the slightest crunch still left in them. If there seems to be a lot of liquid left in the pot, let it simmer uncovered until the excess liquid evaporates, 5 minutes more.

4 Stir in the sunflower cream from the blender and heat it gently. Season with salt.

5 Bring a pot of salted water to a boil. Add the asparagus, reduce the heat to low, and simmer for about 2 minutes, then add the peas and simmer for 2 minutes more, being careful not to overcook them. Drain and rinse the vegetables with cold water.

6 To serve, place about a quarter of the risotto on each plate, then top with the vegetables. Drizzle with olive oil, top with parsley and a sprinkling of flaky sea salt, and serve with lemon wedges.

COOL IT NOODLE SALAD

with Radishes and Peas

SPICY TAHINI GINGER SAUCE

½ cup / 125ml tahini

2 tablespoons grated peeled fresh ginger

2 tablespoons gluten-free tamari or soy sauce

2 teaspoons pure maple syrup or raw honey

1 tablespoon freshly squeezed lime juice

NOODLE SALAD

9 ounces / 250g dried whole-grain pasta

1 cup / 150g green peas, fresh or frozen

2 medium carrots, julienned

7 ounces / 200g (1 small bunch) radishes, sliced

⅓ packed cup / 15g chopped fresh cilantro, for garnish

Sesame Salt, for serving (page 157)

When summer heats up, heaven bless the cold noodle salad! I like to make a big batch of this and keep it in the fridge for when hunger strikes and the last thing I want to do is turn on the stove to boil water. (Tip: Make this in the morning!) Any vegetables work well here, and you can easily adapt this for any time of the year . . . you could even serve it hot.

Although I would traditionally use rice noodles for this dish, it can be difficult to find brown rice noodles at mainstream grocery stores, so I opt for the whole-grain pasta instead. The sauce is a riff on peanut sauce, with ginger, lime, and maple syrup for sweetness. Although you can substitute peanut butter for the tahini, the latter is a healthier option.

SERVES 4 ——————————————————————

1 Make the sauce: Place the tahini, ginger, tamari, maple syrup, lime juice, and ½ cup / 125 ml of water in a blender and blend on high until smooth and creamy. Taste and adjust the seasonings, if necessary. Set aside.

2 Prepare the noodle salad: Bring a pot of heavily salted water to a boil. Add the pasta and cook until just less than al dente, according to the package directions. Add the peas to the boiling water, remove from the heat, and let it sit for 1 minute. Drain and rinse with cold water.

3 In a large serving bowl, toss the pasta and peas with the carrots and radishes. Pour about three quarters of the sauce over top and toss to combine. Divide the noodles among four bowls and garnish with cilantro, more sauce if desired, and Sesame Salt.

ROLLOVER Make double the Spicy Tahini Ginger Sauce for the Run Wild Summer Rolls (page 101).

QUINOA AND BLACK BEANS

with Radish Cilantro Salsa

6 large carrots

2 garlic cloves

1 tablespoon coconut oil or ghee, melted

2 pinches plus ¼ teaspoon fine sea salt

½ cup / 85g quinoa, soaked if possible

Scant 1 cup / 250ml water

1½ cups / 250g (1 15-oz. can) black beans, drained and rinsed

1 tablespoon cold-pressed olive oil

Juice of 1 lime

1 teaspoon crushed red pepper flakes

Radish Cilantro Salsa (recipe follows)

Hot sauce, for serving (optional)

This one-bowl wonder combines southwestern flavors with the surprising freshness and crunch of radishes bathed in lime and cilantro. This salsa can be made a day in advance, but it should be dressed right before serving. It is delicious folded into smashed avocado for a twist on guacamole, or even paired with hummus in a wrap or pita. You'll notice it appears several times in the book since it is easy to make and incredibly versatile. This is a great dish to whip up when you have leftover quinoa and black beans. Serve it with your favorite hot sauce for an extra kick!

SERVES 4 ————————————————————————

1 Preheat the oven to 400°F / 200°C. Scrub the carrots and slice them on the diagonal, about ½ inch / 1.3cm thick. Mince the garlic. Place the carrots and garlic in a single layer on a rimmed baking sheet, drizzle with the coconut oil, and toss to coat. Roast until tender and blistered, about 20 minutes. Remove them from the oven, season with the 2 pinches of salt, and set aside.

2 While the carrots are roasting, cook the quinoa. Rinse the grains and drain them well. Place the quinoa in a small saucepan with the water and ¼ teaspoon of salt. Bring to a boil, reduce the heat to low, and cook, covered, until all the water has been absorbed and the grains are tender, about 20 minutes.

3 In a large serving dish, combine the cooked quinoa and black beans with the olive oil and lime juice. Toss and season with more salt and the pepper flakes. Fold in the carrots and garlic.

(recipe continues)

4 Place a large mound of the Radish Cilantro Salsa on top of the salad, or allow your guests to help themselves. Garnish with more pepper flakes and hot sauce, if desired.

ROLLOVER Cook double the black beans to use in a Stuffed Sweet Potato (page 95).

1½ cups / 225g finely diced radishes

1½ teaspoons minced red onion or shallot

½ cup / 15g chopped fresh cilantro

2 to 3 teaspoons minced red chile (serrano is a good choice)

DRESSING

3 tablespoons freshly squeezed lime juice

3 tablespoons cold-pressed olive oil

1 tablespoon pure maple syrup

2 pinches of fine sea salt, plus more as needed

RADISH CILANTRO SALSA

MAKES ABOUT 1 CUP / 250ML

1 In a medium bowl, combine the radishes, red onion, cilantro, and chile.

2 Make the dressing: In a small bowl, whisk together the lime juice, olive oil, maple syrup, and salt. Just before serving, pour the dressing over the vegetables, fold to combine, and season with more salt as desired.

CHICKPEA CURRY SALAD SANDWICH

It's time to make a case for mayonnaise. I know what you're thinking: how could a nutritionist be championing such an unhealthy food?! But let's look at what mayo actually is: it's primarily just oil and an egg. Do you think oil and eggs are unhealthy? If they are of high quality, then I certainly don't! The nutritional benefits and flavor of your mayonnaise are 100 percent dependent on the quality of the things you make it with, and making mayo at home allows you to control these things. Use only the highest-quality cold-pressed olive oil here (for tips on how to buy olive oil, see page 230), and choose the best eggs you can find.

Needing a seriously awesome vehicle for this mayo, and inspired by the chicken salad sandwiches of my youth, I came up with this vegetarian version that will knock your socks off.

MAKES 8 TO 10 SANDWICHES

1 Make the dressing: In a small bowl, whisk together the mayonnaise, curry powder, lemon juice, and salt and pepper. Season with more salt, if necessary.

2 Make the salad: In a food processor, pulse the chickpeas to roughly chop them—do not overprocess or you'll end up with chickpea purée. You can also do this step by hand.

3 Chop the pecans and raisins, then dice the celery and onions.

4 In a large bowl, combine the chopped chickpeas with the dressing. Add the pecans, raisins, celery, and onions and fold to combine. Season with salt. Enjoy the salad on bread with lettuce and onion slices, if desired.

CURRY DRESSING

6 tablespoons / 90 ml Divine and Foolproof Mayonnaise (recipe follows)

1 tablespoon curry powder

1½ teaspoons freshly squeezed lemon juice

Fine sea salt and freshly ground pepper

SALAD

3 cups / 450g (2 15-oz. cans) cooked chickpeas, drained and rinsed

1 ounce / 30g raw pecans

3 tablespoons raisins

1 stalk celery

2 spring onions

FOR SERVING

6 to 8 slices of whole-grain bread (sourdough if possible)

Crisp lettuce or sprouts

Sliced red onion or shallots (optional)

(recipe continues)

DIVINE AND FOOLPROOF MAYONNAISE

MAKES ABOUT 1 CUP /250 ML

1 egg, at room temperature

1 teaspoon Dijon mustard

2 pinches of fine sea salt

1 tablespoon freshly squeezed lemon juice

¾ cup / 175ml cold-pressed olive oil

1 Crack the egg into the bottom of a wide-mouth jar. Add the mustard, salt, lemon juice, and olive oil.

2 Cover the entire egg with the head of an immersion blender (*Note:* this will not work with an upright blender) and blend on medium speed. When you can see that the mixture has thickened and turned white at the bottom of the jar, slowly move the blender up, waiting for the oil to be incorporated as you go, until you get the texture of mayonnaise.

3 Use immediately; refrigerate leftovers in an airtight jar for up to 1 month. The mayonnaise will thicken slightly once it has cooled in the fridge.

SMOKED LENTIL TACOS

with Pico de Gallo

PICO DE GALLO

1½ cups /250g diced cherry tomatoes

⅓ cup / 65g minced white onion

1 teaspoon minced red chile (serrano is a good choice)

2 tablespoons freshly squeezed lime juice

¼ cup / 7g chopped fresh cilantro leaves and tender stems

Fine sea salt

FILLING

1 cup / 210g green lentils, soaked for 8 hours or up to overnight, if possible

1 tablespoon coconut oil

3 small yellow onions, sliced

1 teaspoon fine sea salt

1 large garlic clove, minced

1.2 ounces / 35g sun-dried tomatoes, chopped

1 teaspoon smoked hot paprika (ground chipotle would also work)

1½ teaspoons dried oregano

2 teaspoons gluten-free tamari or soy sauce

FOR SERVING

6 corn tortillas

Spicy Lime Slaw (page 99)

1 ripe avocado, sliced

Hot sauce (optional)

I haven't eaten any kind of meat in a very long time, but taking my first bite of these insanely tasty tacos made me feel as if I were. You see, meat contains ample amounts of glutamate, an amino acid that is responsible for umami, the taste of yummy savory-ness that helps us feel satisfied. In an attempt to make tacos that lacked for nothing, I knew I had to infuse a ton of mouthwatering flavors into the lentils, so I used my secret weapons: sun-dried tomatoes, tamari, and caramelized onions. The smokiness that we often associate with meat comes from the addition of smoked paprika—genius spice to have in your meat-free arsenal.

MAKES 6 TACOS

1 Make the Pico de Gallo: In a small bowl, combine the cherry tomatoes, onion, chile, lime juice, and cilantro. Season with salt and set aside.

2 Prepare the filling: In a stockpot, combine the lentils and enough water to cover them with water. Bring to a boil, reduce the heat to low, and cook, covered, until tender, about 20 minutes. Drain and rinse them well.

3 Meanwhile, in a skillet, melt the coconut oil over medium-high heat. Add the onions and salt, stir to coat, and cook until the onions soften and begin to slightly caramelize, about 10 minutes. Add the garlic, sun-dried tomatoes, paprika, oregano, and tamari. Stir to coat, adding a little water if the pot is too dry. Cook until fragrant, 2 to 3 minutes, then add the lentils and stir well to incorporate. Taste and season with salt, if necessary, and remove from the heat.

4 To assemble, divide the smoky lentil mixture among the tortillas, followed by the slaw and Pico de Gallo. Add the avocado and hot sauce, if desired.

ROLLOVER Make a double batch of Pico de Gallo and use it in the Quinoa and Black Beans with Radish Cilantro Salsa (page 106) instead of the Radish Cilantro Salsa.

EGGPLANT CANNELLONI

with Sunflower Feta and Toasted Garlic Tomato Sauce

2 large eggplants

1 teaspoon coconut oil

½ teaspoon fine sea salt

TOASTED GARLIC TOMATO SAUCE

¼ cup / 60ml cold-pressed olive oil

3 garlic cloves, minced

½ to 1 teaspoon crushed red pepper flakes

½ teaspoon fine sea salt

1 28-oz. / 794g can crushed tomatoes

FILLING

½ cup / 80g kalamata olives

Generous handful of fresh basil leaves

1 cup / 250 g Sunflower Meta Feta (page 76)

Fine sea salt

ROLLOVER Make enough meta feta to use in the **Tomatoes with Basil and Sunflower Meta Feta (page 76)**.

This recipe for cannelloni skips the pasta and uses roasted eggplant slices instead, making my version lighter and also grain-free. The filling is made from sunflower feta mixed with lemon zest and olives, so it is vegan as well as well as gluten-free; it's also super bright and totally satisfying. The sunflower feta recipe makes more than you'll need here, but you can use it for many things, so make a big batch and get creative!

SERVES 4 —————————————————————————

1 Preheat the oven to 400°F / 200°C.

2 Slice the eggplants lengthwise into long, thin strips (about ¼ inch / 0.5cm thick; you should end up with at least 12 slices). Rub the eggplant slices with the coconut oil and sprinkle with the sea salt. Lay them on a rimmed baking sheet lined with parchment paper.

3 Roast the eggplant slices for 10 minutes, flip them, then roast until soft and browned, 5 to 10 minutes more. Remove from the oven and let cool slightly.

4 Meanwhile, make the sauce: In a medium saucepan, warm the olive oil over low heat. Add the garlic and let lightly simmer until golden, about 1 minute, being careful not to let the oil smoke or the garlic burn. Add the pepper flakes, salt, and tomatoes; stir well. Taste and adjust the seasonings, if necessary. Remove from the heat and set aside, covered, until ready to serve.

5 Make filling: Remove the pits from the olives and roughly chop. Tear the basil leaves. Mix together the meta feta, olives, and basil. Season with salt.

6 Place about 2 tablespoons of the filling at one end of an eggplant slice. Roll it up and place it back on the baking sheet, seam-side down. Repeat with the remaining filling and slices. Return the eggplant to the oven to warm, if desired.

7 To serve, ladle about one quarter of the sauce onto each plate. Top with at least 3 eggplant rolls, drizzle with olive oil, and sprinkle with extra pepper flakes, if desired.

WARMING CHICKPEA MUSHROOM RAGOUT

with Crispy Sage

Ragout is just a fancy French word for "stew," so there's no need to be intimidated by this dish at all. In fact, its ingredients are wholeheartedly humble, and I love tucking into this simple meal on a cold winter's night; it'll warm you from head to toe. Or serve it with a poached egg on top for a lovely weekend breakfast. As much as I like eating this ragout on brown rice, polenta is another wonderful option. Also, it's important not to wash the mushrooms—they will absorb water, and their flavor will be diluted. Instead, brush them clean with a damp paper towel to remove any soil or debris.

SERVES 3 TO 4

1 In a medium saucepan with a tight-fitting lid, combine the rice, water, and ¾ teaspoon of the salt. Bring to a boil, reduce the heat to low, and simmer, covered, until the rice is tender and has absorbed the water, 45 to 50 minutes. If the rice is not yet cooked and needs more water, add about ¼ cup / 60ml of water and continue cooking.

2 Meanwhile, chop the onions and mince the garlic. Melt 1 tablespoon of the coconut oil in a large stockpot over medium heat. Add the onions and the remaining teaspoon of salt, stir to coat, and cook until the onions soften and begin to slightly caramelize, about 10 minutes (add a little broth if the pot becomes too dry). Add the garlic, chopped sage, rosemary, thyme, and mushrooms. Turn the heat to high and cook, stirring every so often, until the mushrooms have released their liquid and softened, about 10 minutes. Add the remaining broth, milk, vinegar, black pepper, and chickpeas. Lower the heat and simmer until the liquid has reduced and thickened slightly.

1 cup / 200g brown rice

2 cups / 500ml water

1¾ teaspoons fine sea salt, plus more for sprinkling

3 medium yellow onions

3 garlic cloves

2 tablespoons coconut oil or ghee

½ cup / 125ml vegetable broth

⅓ cup / 10g fresh sage leaves, roughly chopped, plus 16 more for frying

1½ teaspoons dried rosemary

1½ teaspoons dried thyme

14 ounces / 400g cremini mushrooms, sliced into quarters

½ cup / 125ml plant-based milk of your choice

1 tablespoon balsamic vinegar

1 teaspoon freshly ground black pepper

1½ cups / 225g (1 15-oz. can) cooked chickpeas, drained and rinsed

1½ teaspoons freshly squeezed lemon juice

2 packed cups / 50g spinach leaves

(recipe continues)

3 In a small skillet, melt the remaining tablespoon of coconut oil over medium-high. When hot, add 6 to 8 whole sage leaves at a time and fry them for 10 to 15 seconds. Using a fork, transfer the leaves to paper towels and immediately sprinkle with sea salt. Repeat with the remaining leaves.

4 Remove the ragout from the heat and stir in the lemon juice and spinach leaves just before serving over the rice. Top each plate with 4 crispy sage leaves.

ROLLOVER Cook double the brown rice to make a meal out of the Kale, Mushrooms, and Walnuts with Pecorino (page 158).

PORTOBELLO PIZZAS

Although I am not emotionally equipped to live in a world without traditional pizza, this is a really great alternative if you are looking to fill up on more vegetables instead of grains or starches. Marinated mushrooms create a mega-flavored base for caramelized onions, garlicky spinach, and caper-spiked tomatoes. Although there is a generous cheese mountain on top of these guys, they are delicious without it, if you want the dish to be vegan. Although the recipe yields one mushroom per person, if you have a big appetite (or you are as gluttonous as I am), you may want to make extra!

MAKES 6 PIZZAS ———————————————

1 Using a clean, damp kitchen towel, brush the mushroom caps well, carefully removing any dirt. Remove the stems, roughly chop them, and set aside.

2 In a large resealable plastic bag, combine the vinegar, thyme, oregano, rosemary, 3 of the minced garlic cloves, and ½ teaspoon of the salt, smooshing and sloshing the mixture a bit to incorporate. Place the whole mushroom caps in the bag, seal it up, roll the contents around to coat them with the marinade, and let it sit in the fridge for a minimum of 30 minutes, or up to 3 hours. If you think of it, take the bag out from time to time and roll it around to ensure that the mushrooms are well covered with the marinade.

3 In a large skillet, melt the coconut oil over medium-high heat. Add the onions, chopped mushroom stems, and the remaining ½ teaspoon of salt, and toss to coat. Cook, stirring often, until the onions soften and are fully caramelized, about 20 minutes. Add a little water to the pan if it becomes dry.

6 large portobello mushrooms

¼ cup / 60ml balsamic vinegar

1½ teaspoons dried thyme

1½ teaspoons dried oregano

1½ teaspoons dried rosemary

4 garlic cloves, minced

1 teaspoon fine sea salt

1 tablespoon coconut oil or ghee

3 medium yellow onions, sliced

4 packed cups / 100g baby spinach leaves

½ pound / 225g tomatoes

⅓ cup / 50g capers, rinsed

Freshly ground black pepper

Pecorino Romano, for garnish (optional; Parmesan will also work)

Handful of fresh basil leaves, for garnish (optional)

(recipe continues)

4 Transfer the caramelized onions to a bowl without cleaning the pan. Add the remaining minced garlic clove and spinach to the pan with a small splash of water. Increase the heat to high and wilt the spinach, stirring often, until it is dark green and soft, 1 to 2 minutes, being careful not to overcook.

5 Chop the tomatoes and combine them with the capers and black pepper in a small bowl.

6 Preheat the oven to 400°F / 200°C. Assemble the mushroom caps by placing them top-side down on a rimmed baking sheet lined with parchment paper. Spoon about one sixth of the caramelized onions onto each mushroom. Top each with some wilted spinach, followed by the tomato-caper mixture. You can add some grated cheese at this point if you like, or wait until after the pizzas have come out of the oven.

7 Bake until the mushrooms are heated through, 15 to 20 minutes. Grate the cheese over top and garnish with the basil if desired. Serve hot.

BUTTERNUT SQUASH AND SAGE OVEN RISOTTO

2 tablespoons ghee or coconut oil (preferably ghee)

2 medium yellow onions, finely diced

1 teaspoon fine sea salt

5 to 7 cups / 1.2 to 1.7 liters vegetable broth

4 garlic cloves

15 fresh sage leaves, sliced

2 pounds / 1kg butternut squash, peeled and chopped into ½-inch / 1.3cm cubes

2½ cups / 500g short-grain brown rice, soaked overnight if possible

1 rind of Pecorino Romano

Cold-pressed olive oil, for serving

Freshly grated Pecorino Romano or Parmesan, for serving (optional)

ROLLOVER Save extra sage for the Warming Chickpea Mushroom Ragout with Crispy Sage (page 117).

Risotto intimidates a lot of people, but I think this comes from the sheer notion of commitment: having to stand by the stove for some time, stir the pot constantly, add broth at *just* the right moment, and make sure the rice is neither under- nor overcooked but perfectly al dente. This oven method eliminates pretty much all of that.

Short-grain brown rice is the best rice to use here because it is starchier than long-grain brown rice, which helps to create a creamy consistency. The incredible depth of flavor comes from using a cheese rind. I always save my rinds in the freezer until an occasion such as this comes along. You will not believe how it permeates the entire dish, which means that you need to add very little extra cheese at the end to achieve the deep umami taste we all crave.

SERVES 4 TO 6

1 Preheat the oven to 425°F / 220°C.

2 In a large ovenproof pot fitted with a lid, melt the ghee over medium heat. Add the onions and salt and sauté until translucent and slightly caramelized, about 10 minutes, adding a little broth if the pot becomes too dry. Add the garlic and sage and cook until fragrant, about 2 minutes.

3 Add the butternut squash, rice, 5 cups / 1.2 liters of broth, and the cheese rind to the pot. Stir well, cover the pot, and bake for 20 minutes. Remove from the oven, stir once, and check the liquid levels. If you think that there is not enough broth, add 1 cup / 250ml or so, then cover the pot and put it back in the oven, checking every 15 minutes or so until the rice is tender. It should cook for about 60 minutes if your rice has been soaked, up to 90 minutes if you start with dry rice.

4 Serve hot with a drizzle of olive oil and extra Pecorino Romano grated over top, if desired.

ROLLOVER Double the pesto to serve as a delicious party
dip or a spread for sandwiches or crackers.

VIBRANT PINK
PESTO PASTA

Vibrant food is healthy food! Deep pigments signal powerful nutrients, and there is something so alluring about the rich magenta hue of this pasta dish. The pesto uses roasted beets to attain its bright-pink pigment and cleverly dyes the pasta that it touches, creating a unique and totally unexpected visual. Choose whole-grain pasta for this recipe, and don't worry if it is naturally dark in color; the pesto will undoubtedly shine through—it's powerful stuff! The goat cheese is an optional topping, but it adds a gorgeous, creamy texture and salty counterpoint to the earthy-sweet pesto. If you don't have parsley on hand, basil or mint would also be delicious.

SERVES 4 TO 6 ────────────────

1 Preheat the oven to 400°F / 200°C. Wrap the beets in foil and roast until tender, 40 to 60 minutes. Remove the beets from the oven, unwrap the foil, and let them cool slightly before slipping off the skins.

2 While the beets are roasting, heat a large skillet over medium. Add the pumpkin seeds and lightly toast, stirring occasionally, until fragrant, 3 to 5 minutes. Remove from heat and set aside.

3 In a food processor, pulse the garlic until minced. Roughly chop the beets and add them to the processor along with the pumpkin seeds, lemon juice, olive oil, and salt, and process until relatively smooth. Taste and add more salt and lemon juice as needed.

4 Fill a large pot with water and bring to a boil. Add salt and the pasta and cook until al dente, according to the package directions. Drain, place the pasta back in the pot, and drizzle with olive oil. Stir in the pesto.

5 To serve, divide the cooked pasta among individual plates, crumble the cheese on top, sprinkle with parsley, and season with salt. Garnish with extra olive oil, if desired.

PESTO

1 pound / 450g red beets

⅓ cup / 50 g raw, unsalted pumpkin seeds

2 garlic cloves

1½ teaspoons freshly squeezed lemon juice, plus more as needed

3 tablespoons cold-pressed olive oil

½ teaspoon fine sea salt, plus more as needed

PASTA

Fine sea salt

1⅓ pounds / 600g dried whole-grain pasta of your choice, preferably spaghetti or linguine

Cold-pressed olive oil, for drizzling

7 ounces / 200g soft goat cheese

Fresh flat-leaf parsley, for garnish

ONE-POT CLEANSING KICHADI

3 medium yellow onions

2 medium carrots

1 large tomato

½ cup / 110g mung beans
or brown lentils, soaked if
possible

1 tablespoon coconut oil
or ghee

1½ teaspoons cumin seeds

1½ teaspoons mustard seeds

1½ teaspoons coriander
seeds

½ teaspoon ground turmeric

1 cinnamon stick

1 teaspoon fine sea salt

2 tablespoons peeled,
minced fresh ginger

5 ounces / 150g green
beans, fresh or frozen

1 cup / 200g brown rice,
soaked if possible

1 cup / 150g green peas,
fresh or frozen

2 handfuls of finely chopped
fresh cilantro, for serving

ROLLOVER Turn any leftovers
of this stew into a savory
breakfast the next day with a
poached egg and some stir-
fried greens.

Kichadi, sometimes called and spelled khichdi, kitchari, kitcheree, or khichri, is the famous one-pot Indian dish that combines rice and lentils or quick-cooking pulses such as mung beans. It's best known in Ayurvedic tradition as a complete protein meal; it's also very easy to digest and a cinch to make!

Because of its simplicity and ease, many people find that doing a detox on kichadi is very pleasant and far less of an undertaking than a juice fast, for example. Eating this dish exclusively for three to five days is said to purify the digestive organs while cleansing the body of toxins. I like to do this in the winter months when the weather is cold and I need some grounding, warm food and juicing seems out of the question.

Soaking the rice and lentils together overnight is rather important for improving the digestive qualities of kichadi, but if you are pressed for time, you can skip this step.

SERVES 6 TO 8

1 Prepare the vegetables: Dice the onions, and chop the carrots and tomato. Set aside in separate bowls. Drain and rinse the mung beans.

2 In a large stockpot, melt the coconut oil over medium heat. Add the cumin and mustard seeds and fry just until the mustard seeds start to pop. Stir in the coriander, turmeric, cinnamon stick, and salt, then add the ginger and tomato. Cook until fragrant, about 2 minutes.

3 Add the onions, carrots, green beans, rice, mung beans, peas, and 4 cups / 1 liter of water. Bring to a boil, reduce the heat to low, and simmer, covered, until the rice and beans are soft, about 45 minutes. Add more water if the pot becomes dry while cooking or to achieve a more stew-like consistency.

4 Season with salt and serve with the cilantro.

SWEET POTATO, CAULIFLOWER, AND COCONUT CASSEROLE

Perhaps they're a tad retro, but casseroles are undeniably comforting. This one features a unique combination of sweet potatoes, cauliflower, and coconut milk steeped in warming spices, and a satisfying crunchy nut topping. To change things up a little, simply try a different spice blend, or use dried herbs instead, such as rosemary and thyme. Serve this with a fresh green salad on the side for extra nutrients and to complement the warming, grounding nature of the casserole.

SERVES 6

1 Preheat the oven to 400°F / 200°C. In a small bowl, whisk together the coconut milk, tamari, spices, and a few pinches of salt.

2 Make the topping: In a food processor, pulse the almonds, sunflower seeds, oats, ½ teaspoon salt, and pepper until crumbly. Add the coconut oil and 2 tablespoons of the coconut milk mixture and pulse until it holds together when pressed.

3 Cut the sweet potato and cauliflower into ⅓-inch- / 8mm-thick slices. Alternating between sweet potato and cauliflower, layer the slices horizontally in a 9 x 13-inch / 23 x 33cm baking pan, seasoning with more salt as you go. Stuff leftover pieces of cauliflower in the spaces between the vegetables.

4 Pour the coconut milk mixture over the vegetables. Spread the almond topping over top, squeezing a few bits of it together here and there so that you create some chunks. Cover the dish with foil, making sure to seal the sides.

5 Bake until the vegetables are tender but not mushy, 30 to 35 minutes, then remove the foil and continue baking until the topping browns, 10 minutes more. Garnish with fresh parsley, if desired. Serve hot.

1 14-oz. can full-fat coconut milk

1 tablespoon gluten-free tamari or soy sauce

¼ teaspoon each ground cloves, cardamom, and freshly grated nutmeg

½ teaspoon fine sea salt, plus more as needed

½ cup / 75g raw, unsalted almonds

½ cup / 80g raw, unsalted, shelled sunflower seeds

1 cup / 100g gluten-free rolled oats

1 teaspoon freshly ground black pepper

2 tablespoons coconut oil

1 large / 500g sweet potato, unpeeled

1 head of cauliflower

Handful of fresh flat-leaf parsley or fresh cilantro leaves, for garnish (optional)

SAVORY LEEK AND MUSHROOM GALETTE

DOUGH

2 cups / 300g whole-grain wheat flour

½ cup / 50g rolled oats

¼ teaspoon fine sea salt

Scant ½ cup / 115ml coconut oil, cold

¾ cup / 185ml ice water

FILLING

1 tablespoon ghee or coconut oil

4 cups / 350g chopped leeks, white and light-green parts only

1 teaspoon fine sea salt

3 garlic cloves, minced

1 tablespoon dried thyme

1 teaspoon freshly ground black pepper

3 large portobello mushrooms, sliced

2 packed cups / 50g baby spinach leaves

1 tablespoon freshly squeezed lemon juice

3½ ounces / 100g feta cheese (preferably goat or sheep)

Fresh flat-leaf parsley leaves, for garnish (optional)

If pastry intimidates you, behold the galette. Easy to make and hard to mess up, this foolproof tart can be mastered by anyone. Although one would normally think of this as a sweet dessert, this recipe is deliciously savory and makes a main dish far more impressive than the effort that went into it. The filling is a richly seasoned combination of creamy leeks and mushrooms with an honest dose of spinach that cleverly melts into the mix and doesn't overwhelm. The crust is hearty and satisfying, with crunchy edges that complement the tender filling. If you would prefer a vegan dish, simply leave out the feta cheese and use coconut oil instead of ghee.

SERVES 4 TO 6 ────────────────

1 Prepare the dough: Place the flour, oats, and salt in a large bowl and stir to combine. Cut the cold coconut oil into pieces and add it to the bowl. Use a pastry cutter or a couple of forks to cut the oil into the flour until the mixture has a pealike consistency. Drizzle in about 5 tablespoons of the ice water and continue to mix the ingredients until a small amount of it holds together when squeezed. You may need to add more water, up to ¾ cup / 185ml. Do not overwork the dough or add too much water or the crust will be tough and chewy.

2 Gather the dough into a rough ball in the bowl, then transfer it to a piece of plastic wrap. Wrap the dough ball in plastic and flatten it into a rough disk. Chill the dough in the fridge for at least an hour and up to 2 days.

(recipe continues)

3 Make the filling: In a large skillet, melt the ghee over medium-high heat. Add the leeks and salt, stir to coat, and cook until the leeks soften and are slightly caramelized, about 10 minutes. Add the garlic, thyme, pepper, and mushrooms, stir to coat, and cook until the mushrooms have softened, 5 to 7 minutes. Remove from the heat, add the spinach and lemon juice, and stir until the spinach has wilted.

4 Preheat the oven to 400°F / 200°C.

5 Remove the dough from the plastic wrap. Place it between 2 large pieces of parchment paper, and roll it out into a 14-inch/ 36cm round. Peel off the top piece of parchment.

6 Add the filling to the dough disk and spread it evenly, leaving a 2-inch / 5cm space around the edges. Crumble the feta over the top and fold about 1½ inches / 4cm of the crust's edge over onto the filling all around. Slide the parchment paper with the galette onto a rimmed baking sheet and bake until the crust is golden and cooked through, 35 to 40 minutes.

7 Slice the galette into wedges, sprinkle with parsley, if desired, and enjoy hot or at room temperature.

ROLLOVER Double the dough recipe, freeze half, and make a galette next season using totally different produce. This would be lovely with a filling of mixed roasted veggies, such as pumpkin, beets, and sweet potatoes.

GRILLED EGGPLANT AND MUSHROOMS

with Saucy Almond Butter Noodles

There is something undeniably satisfying about a big noodle bowl smothered in delicious sauce and piled high with colorful veggies. It's the kind of thing I'm in the mood for any time of year. I really like grilling the eggplant and mushrooms, but you can also roast them in the oven if you don't feel like firing up the barbecue, or if you don't have a grill pan. If you're feeling ambitious, make a batch of the Ginger-Pickled Carrots (page 87) to serve here; their tender crunch and bright acidity really round out the dish.

SERVES 4

2 medium eggplants

4 portobello mushrooms, stems removed

¼ cup / 35g raw, unsalted sesame seeds

½ pound / 250g dried rice noodles (preferably brown rice noodles)

Almond Butter Sauce (recipe follows)

Ginger-Pickled Carrots (optional, but delicious; page 87)

¼ packed cup / 10g chopped fresh cilantro

1 Preheat your grill to high. Slice the eggplants into ½-inch / 1.3cm rounds and the mushrooms into ¼-inch/ 0.5cm slices. Place the vegetables on the grill and cook until softened and marked on the underside, about 5 minutes. Flip and grill on the other side until the vegetables are softened and charred, 3 to 4 minutes more.

2 Preheat a small dry skillet over medium heat. When hot, toast the sesame seeds, stirring frequently, until fragrant, 2 to 3 minutes. Immediately remove the pan from the heat and set it aside.

3 Fill a medium saucepan with water and bring to a boil. Add the rice noodles and cook until tender, according to the package directions. Drain and set aside.

4 To serve, place about a quarter of the noodles on each plate. Top with grilled veggies and pour the Almond Butter Sauce over top. Garnish with Ginger-Pickled Carrots, if desired, cilantro, and sesame seeds.

(recipe continues)

ALMOND BUTTER SAUCE

MAKES ABOUT 1 CUP / 250ML

In a blender, combine the almond butter, garlic, tamari, maple syrup, ginger, lime juice, chile, and water, and blend until smooth and creamy. Taste and season with salt, if necessary.

ROLLOVER Make an extra batch of Almond Butter Sauce and use it for the Run Wild Summer Rolls (page 101).

½ cup / 125ml almond butter

2 small garlic cloves

2 tablespoons gluten-free tamari or soy sauce

1 tablespoon pure maple syrup

½ teaspoon peeled, minced fresh ginger

6 tablespoons freshly squeezed lime juice (from approximately 2 limes)

1 small red chile, stem and seeds removed (serrano is a good choice)

½ cup / 125ml water

Sea salt

BUTTER BEAN GINGER STEW

1 tablespoon coconut oil
or ghee

2½ cups / 250g chopped
leeks, white and light-green
parts only (onions will also
work)

Fine sea salt

2 teaspoons ground turmeric

Pinch of cayenne pepper

3 bay leaves

5 garlic cloves, sliced

1½ teaspoons peeled,
minced fresh ginger

4 medium carrots, scrubbed

1 14-oz. can whole peeled
tomatoes

2½ cups / 625ml vegetable
broth

3 lemon slices

1½ teaspoons pure maple
syrup

1½ cups / 225g (1 15-oz.
can) cooked butter beans
(any white bean will work),
drained and rinsed

2 packed cups / 50g baby
spinach leaves

Cold-pressed olive oil, for
serving

Freshly ground black pepper,
for serving

Butter beans undoubtedly live up to their name: deliciously creamy and melt-in-your-mouth tender. Instead of blending them up to make a dip (which would be a shame!), I enjoy them in soups, stews, and salads, where I can really get the most out of their impressive size and unique texture. In this simple, nourishing recipe, butter beans are combined with stewed tomatoes and carrots, warming ginger, turmeric, and cayenne, with a touch of lemon for brightness. Instead of cooking the spinach, you'll add it right before serving so that it just wilts, retaining many of its delicate nutrients. Make a double batch of this and freeze leftovers for a perfect heat-and-eat meal when you're tempted to order takeout!

SERVES 3 TO 4

1 In a large stockpot, melt the coconut oil over medium heat. Add the leeks and a couple of pinches of salt, the turmeric, cayenne, and bay leaves. Cook until the leeks have softened, about 5 minutes, then add the garlic and ginger. If the pot becomes dry, add a little liquid from the canned tomatoes.

2 Slice the carrots in quarters lengthwise and then in half across their width so that you end up with batons. Add the carrots, tomatoes and their liquid, vegetable broth, lemon slices, and maple syrup to the pot. Bring to a boil, reduce the heat to low, and simmer until the carrots are tender but not mushy, 15 to 20 minutes.

3 Add the cooked butter beans to the pot, stir, and let them heat through, 3 to 4 minutes. Remove from the heat and fold in the spinach—it will wilt from the residual heat. Serve with a drizzle of olive oil and a few grinds of black pepper.

ROLLOVER Make this stew even more substantial by serving it on top of Copycat Couscous with Clementines (page 175).

SPROUTED LENTIL CHILI

1 tablespoon coconut oil or ghee

2 medium yellow onions, diced

1 medium leek, white and light-green parts only, diced

1 teaspoon fine sea salt, plus more as needed

5 garlic cloves, minced

1½ teaspoons ground cumin

1½ teaspoons ground coriander

1 teaspoon ground cinnamon

½ teaspoon ground chipotle

1 small red chile (stem and seeds removed), sliced (serrano is a good choice)

1.7 ounces / 50g sun-dried tomatoes (about 8), roughly chopped

1 medium red bell pepper (stem, seeds, and ribs removed), diced

1 pound / 500g sweet potatoes and/or carrots, diced

1 14-oz. can diced tomatoes

2½ cups / 625ml vegetable broth

2 cups / 170g lentil sprouts (see Basic Sprouts, page 23)

Here's a fun take on classic chili—using sprouted lentils instead of beans. The result is a much lighter chili that leaves you feeling satisfied but not stuffed. The sprouted lentils aid digestion and give you a huge boost of protein, fiber, and minerals. Remember that sprouts take about three days to grow, so make sure you start this meal well in advance! If you've never made your own sprouts before, check out the simple instructions on page 23. If you're pressed for time, you can also purchase bean sprouts from the grocery store. The topping for the chili is also delicious on toast or crackers, in a wrap, or simply folded through simple greens for an instant salad.

SERVES 4

1 In a large stockpot, melt the coconut oil over medium heat. Add the onions, leek, and salt, and stir to coat. Cook until the onions soften and begin to slightly caramelize, about 10 minutes. Add the garlic and spices and cook until fragrant, about 2 minutes.

2 Add the chile, sun-dried tomatoes, bell pepper, and sweet potatoes, and cook for 5 minutes more, adding a little broth to the pot if it becomes dry.

3 Add the canned tomatoes with their juices, along with the vegetable broth. Bring to a boil, reduce the heat to low, and cook until the sweet potatoes are tender, 15 to 20 minutes. Remove from heat and keep warm.

4 Meanwhile, make the topping: In a small bowl, combine the 1 cup lentil sprouts, lime juice, salt, olive oil, avocado, and cilantro.

5 Stir the 2 cups sprouted lentils into the chili. Season with salt. Serve in bowls with a scoop of the topping and a drizzle of olive oil.

TOPPING

1 cup / 85g lentil sprouts (see Basic Sprouts, page 23)

Juice of ½ lime

Pinch of fine sea salt

1 tablespoon cold-pressed olive oil, plus more for serving

1 ripe avocado, cubed

Small handful of fresh cilantro, roughly chopped

POLENTA

with Beet Ribbons and Arugula Pesto

If you're looking to serve something impressive and restaurant-worthy to guests, this dish is sure to fit the bill. Creamy polenta, rich arugula pesto, and sweet, earthy beets combine to create a harmonious, not to mention beautiful, meal. By simply slicing the roasted beets into thin ribbons and curling them around each other, you'll end up with such a spectacular presentation that it will look like you've been to culinary school.

There are three elements to this dish, but both the roasted beets and the pesto can be made up to three days ahead of time, so all you have to do before serving is cook the polenta, making this very doable on a weeknight when you want to put something special on the table.

SERVES 4 ────────────────

1 Preheat the oven to 400°F / 200°C. Wrap the beets in foil and place them on a rimmed baking sheet. Roast for about 45 minutes. The beets are ready when you can easily insert a sharp knife into the center. Remove them from the oven, peel back the foil a little, and let them cool. When the beets are cool, slip the skins off.

2 While the beets are roasting, make the polenta. In a large saucepan, heat the vegetable broth and a good pinch of salt until it begins to simmer. Slowly pour in the polenta in a steady stream, whisking all the while to prevent clumping. Whisk constantly for a couple of minutes, then reduce the heat to low and cover the saucepan. Stir every 5 minutes or so until the polenta is creamy without any grit to it, 30 to 45 minutes total. If the polenta becomes too thick, whisk in a little hot water or more vegetable broth.

3 While the polenta is cooking, make the pesto: Lower the oven temperature to 350°F / 180°C.

GF

2 medium red beets

4 to 6 cups / 1 to 1.5 liters vegetable broth or salted water

Fine sea salt

1 cup / 160g polenta (cornmeal)

ARUGULA PESTO

½ cup / 50g raw, unsalted walnuts

1 small garlic clove

2 packed cups / 50g arugula

1 ounce / 30g Pecorino Romano, freshly grated (about 6 tablespoons; Parmesan will also work)

1 tablespoon freshly squeezed lemon juice

2 tablespoons cold-pressed olive oil

Fine sea salt

3½ ounces / 100g feta (preferably sheep or goat)

1 tablespoon cold-pressed olive oil, for drizzling

Flaky sea salt and freshly ground black pepper, for serving

(recipe continues)

4 Place the walnuts on a rimmed baking sheet and toast them in the oven for 7 to 10 minutes, watching them so they do not burn. Remove from the oven and let cool slightly.

5 In a food processor, pulse the garlic until minced. Add the walnuts and pulse to mince. Add the arugula, Pecorino, lemon juice, and olive oil, and pulse until uniform. Season with salt. (The pesto will keep in an airtight container in the fridge for up to 3 days.)

6 Place the peeled beets on a cutting board and slice off the ends. Using a vegetable peeler, slice the beets into strips. Set aside.

7 To assemble, spoon about a quarter of the polenta onto each plate and top each with the desired amount of pesto. Roll up the beet ribbons and sink them down into the pesto and polenta. Curl more beet pieces in and around the rolls until most of the polenta is covered. Crumble the feta over top, drizzle with olive oil, and sprinkle with salt and pepper.

ROLLOVER Spread leftover pesto on toasted whole-grain bread and top with a poached egg.

CEREMONIAL STUFFED PUMPKIN

with Bulgur, Feta, and Figs

This is celebration food: a dish to gather friends and family and one that marks an occasion. Serve this stuffed pumpkin at an autumn harvest or throughout the holiday season for an impressive centerpiece that will tell everyone at your table how much you care. There is a bit of everything going on in this meal, which is why it is so darn delicious. Sweet roasted pumpkin, chewy bulgur, lemony kale, salty feta, crispy pumpkin seeds, chewy dried figs, and sharp onion—a deluge of tastes and textures! If you cannot find bulgur, use brown rice or whole wheat couscous instead. I like to massage the kale for a couple of minutes before adding the remaining ingredients. This step is optional, but it's a simple, cool trick that creates a much sweeter and tenderer green!

SERVES 4

1 cup / 175g bulgur

½ teaspoon fine sea salt, plus more as needed

1 garlic clove, finely minced

1 tablespoon cold-pressed olive oil, plus more for massaging the kale

1 tablespoon freshly squeezed lemon juice

1 small (about 3-pound / 1.5kg) pumpkin or winter squash, such as Hokkaido or acorn

Coconut oil or ghee, for rubbing the pumpkin

1 Rinse the bulgur well and place it in a pot with 2 cups / 500ml of water and the salt. Bring to a boil, reduce the heat to low, and cook, covered, until the grains are tender but still a little al dente, 25 to 35 minutes. Immediately stir in the garlic, olive oil, and lemon juice while the bulgur is still hot, and season with more sea salt, if desired. Remove from heat and re-cover so the grains stay warm.

2 While the bulgur is cooking, roast the pumpkin. Preheat the oven to 400°F / 200°C. Wash the outside of the pumpkin thoroughly—you will be eating the skin as well as the flesh. Slice around the stem, including a good amount of flesh; this will be your "lid." Scoop out the seeds. Rub the inside, outside, and the lid with a little coconut oil or ghee. Place the pumpkin with its lid on a rimmed baking sheet and roast for 25 to 30 minutes. The pumpkin is cooked when a knife can be easily inserted into the flesh.

(recipe continues)

FILLING

4 firmly packed cups /
120g shredded kale

1 tablespoon cold-pressed
olive oil

1 tablespoon freshly
squeezed lemon juice

½ teaspoon fine sea salt

¼ cup / 30g raw, unsalted
pumpkin seeds

1½ cups / 225g (1 15-oz.
can) cooked chickpeas,
drained and rinsed

4 large dried figs
(2.5 ounces / 75g),
roughly chopped

1 small red onion or
2 shallots, thinly sliced

A few pinches of crushed red
pepper flakes (optional)

⅔ cup / 80g crumbled feta
(preferably goat or sheep)

3 Meanwhile, pepare the filling: In a large bowl, combine the kale, the olive oil, lemon juice, and salt. Using your hands, rub and squeeze the kale together as if you are giving it a massage, until the kale leaves are dark green and tender, about 2 minutes.

4 In a dry skillet over medium heat, toast the pumpkin seeds until fragrant, 3 to 5 minutes.

5 In a very large bowl, combine the bulgur, chickpeas, kale, figs, onion, pumpkin seeds, pepper flakes, if using, and feta. Toss to coat and season with salt.

6 To serve, stuff as much of the filling as you can into the pumpkin. Place the lid on the pumpkin, or let the filling spill out onto the platter and serve the lid on the side. Cut the pumpkin into wedges and serve with the filling on top.

ROLLOVER This filling recipe makes enough for 2 stuffed pumpkins or 1 pumpkin with plenty left over; use it to replace the Sunflower Meta Feta in the Eggplant Cannelloni with Sunflower Feta and Toasted Garlic Tomato Sauce (page 114).

WILD RICE, ROASTED CARROT, AND POMEGRANATE BOLD BOWL

This is, quite simply, a bold bowl of yumminess! The nutty flavor from the wild rice pairs so well with the sweetness of carrots and tangy burst of pomegranate seeds. A drizzle of Toasted Walnut Sauce takes it over the top. Serve this bright delight during the holiday season, when pomegranates are ripe and juicy. It can easily be the centerpiece of the meal or a tasty side dish to accompany a feast of other cold-weather favorites.

SERVES 4 ————————————————————————————————

¾ cup / 120g wild rice, soaked overnight if possible

½ teaspoon fine sea salt, plus more as needed

½ pound / 225g carrots, scrubbed

2 teaspoons coconut oil or ghee

1 pomegranate

1 loosely packed cup / 30g fresh flat-leaf parsley leaves

Toasted Walnut Sauce (page 84)

1½ cups / 225g (1 15-oz. can) cooked chickpeas, drained and rinsed

1 Rinse the wild rice, then place it in small saucepan with ½ teaspoon of salt. Cover with plenty of water and bring to a boil. Reduce the heat to low and cook, covered, until the rice is tender and chewy, 45 to 60 minutes.

2 While the rice is cooking, roast the carrots. Preheat the oven to 400°F / 200°C. Slice the carrots lengthwise into halves or quarters, depending on their size, and place them on a rimmed baking sheet with the coconut oil. Place the baking sheet in the oven to melt the coconut oil, remove it from the oven, and toss the carrots to coat, then sprinkle with 2 pinches of sea salt. Return the carrots to the oven and roast until they are blistered and tender, 15 to 20 minutes.

3 Remove the pomegranate seeds from the fruit and roughly chop the parsley. In a large bowl, toss the cooked wild rice with about half of the Toasted Walnut Sauce and the carrots, chickpeas, pomegranate seeds, and parsley. Serve warm or at room temperature with the extra dressing on the side.

ROLLOVER Roast twice as many carrots to make Smoky Roasted Carrot Hummus (page 188).

CAULIFLOWER STEAKS
with Chermoula and Eggs

2 heads of cauliflower

1 tablespoon coconut oil
or ghee

Fine sea salt

CHERMOULA

1 garlic clove

2 pinches of fine sea salt

¼ teaspoon smoked hot
paprika (ground chipotle
would also work)

½ teaspoon freshly ground
black pepper

½ teaspoon crushed red
pepper flakes

1 teaspoon ground cumin

½ teaspoon ground
coriander

¼ cup / 60ml cold-pressed
olive oil

¼ cup / 60ml freshly
squeezed lemon juice

2 packed cups / 60g fresh
flat-leaf parsley leaves, plus
extra for garnish

2 packed cups / 60g fresh
cilantro leaves, plus extra for
garnish

4 to 8 large eggs
(1 or 2 eggs per person)

Chermoula is a spicy flavor bomb of a sauce from North Africa, typically used to marinate meat and fish, but it is wildly delicious with veggies too. Here I've paired it with big slabs of roasted cauliflower and a poached egg, making a substantial and truly satisfying meal. If you can multitask, this dish comes together easily in thirty minutes.

SERVES 4

1 Preheat the oven to 400°F / 200°C. Cut the cauliflower from top to bottom into ½-inch / 1.3cm-thick slices. Save any florets or small pieces for another dish. Rub the cauliflower with the coconut oil and season with salt. Place it on a large rimmed baking sheet and roast until golden and tender but not mushy, 20 to 30 minutes.

2 While the cauliflower is roasting, make the chermoula: In a food processor, pulse the garlic until minced. Add the salt, spices, oil, and lemon juice, and pulse to combine. Roughly chop the herbs, add them, and pulse until the desired consistency is reached—it's delicious smooth or left a little chunky. (This step can be done ahead of time; leftovers keep in an airtight container in the fridge for up to 4 days.)

3 Poach the eggs: Bring a shallow pot of water to a simmer over low heat. Gently stir the water to create a whirlpool. Crack 1 egg into a small dish, then carefully transfer the egg to the center of the whirlpool. Poach the egg for 3 to 4 minutes. Remove the egg from the water with a slotted spoon and place it on a clean kitchen towel to absorb any water. Repeat with the remaining eggs.

4 To serve, place a generous dollop of chermoula (about ¼ cup / 60ml, or more as desired) on each plate, followed by 2 cauliflower steaks. Season the cauliflower with salt, add 1 or 2 poached eggs, and top with a sprinkling of fresh herbs. Enjoy immediately.

ROLLOVER Fold any extra chermoula into warm or cold cooked grains, or use it like a pesto over pasta. I also really love it on toast with an egg for breakfast—a great way to start your day with a download of nourishing herbs!

simple sides and
SMALL PLATES
—

PREVIOUS PAGE, from left to right: Beets and Butter Beans with Lemon and Mint, page 153 / Beets with Avocado, Sesame, and Ginger, page 154 / Balsamic Beets with Hazelnut, Parsley, and Pomegranate, page 155

ROASTED BEETS, 3 WAYS

Roasting beets brings out the incredible depth and sweetness in these roots, giving them a rich, caramelized taste. These three salads show the versatility of roasted beets and their ability to become a blank canvas for so many international flavors. I like to cook a large amount of beets at the beginning of the week to use in a variety of dishes, or I keep them as the star of the show, as in the tantalizing recipes below. Roasted beets will keep in an airtight container in the refrigerator for up to four days.

BEETS AND BUTTER BEANS
with Lemon and Mint

SERVES 3 TO 4 ————————————————————————

1 Preheat the oven to 400°F / 200°C oven. Wrap each beet individually in foil and place them on a rimmed baking sheet. Roast for 30 to 60 minutes, depending on the size of the beets. The beets are ready when you can insert a sharp knife into the center without too much resistance—they should be tender, not mushy. When they are cool enough to handle, peel off and discard the skins, cut the beets into bite-size chunks, and place them in a bowl.

2 Preheat a dry skillet over medium heat. When hot, toast the pumpkin seeds, tossing often, until fragrant, 3 to 5 minutes. Remove the pan from the heat and set aside.

3 In a small bowl, whisk together the olive oil, lemon zest and juice, maple syrup, and a pinch of salt. Pour the dressing over the beets, then fold in the mint, white beans, and pumpkin seeds. Season with salt.

1.7 pounds / 750g beets

¼ cup / 25g raw, unsalted pumpkin seeds

2 tablespoons cold-pressed olive oil

Zest of 1 lemon

2 tablespoons freshly squeezed lemon juice

½ teaspoon pure maple syrup

Fine sea salt

½ cup / 10g chopped fresh mint

1½ cups / 225g (1 15-oz. can) cooked butter beans, drained and rinsed

BEETS

with Avocado, Sesame, and Ginger

1.7 pounds / 750g beets

2 tablespoons raw, unsalted sesame seeds

2 teaspoons peeled, minced fresh ginger

2 tablespoons freshly squeezed lime juice

2 tablespoons cold-pressed olive oil

2 ripe avocados

2 generous pinches of flaky sea salt

SERVES 3 TO 4

1 Preheat the oven to 400°F / 200°C. Wrap each beet individually in foil and place them on a rimmed baking sheet. Roast for 30 to 60 minutes, depending on the size of the beets. The beets are ready when you can insert a sharp knife into the center without too much resistance—they should be tender, not mushy. Remove the beets from the oven, peel back the foil a little, and let them cool. When they are cool enough to handle, peel off and discard the skins, cut the beets into bite-size chunks, and place them in a bowl.

2 Preheat a dry skillet over medium heat. When hot, toast the sesame seeds, stirring frequently, until fragrant and beginning to pop, 2 to 3 minutes. Remove the pan from the heat and set aside.

3 In a small bowl, whisk together the minced ginger, lime juice, and olive oil. Pour this dressing over the beets, add half of the sesame seeds, and fold to combine.

4 To serve, slice the avocados into thin sections and fan them out on a large platter. Spoon the beets over top, sprinkle with the remaining sesame seeds, and season with the salt. Serve immediately.

BALSAMIC BEETS

with Hazelnuts, Parsley, and Pomegranate

SERVES 3 TO 4 ———————————

1 Preheat the oven to 400°F / 200°C. Wrap each beet individually in foil and place them on a rimmed baking sheet. Roast for 30 to 60 minutes, depending on the size of the beets. The beets are ready when you can insert a sharp knife into the center without too much resistance—they should be tender, not mushy. Remove the beets from the oven, peel back the foil a little, and let them cool. When they are cool enough to handle, peel off and discard the skins, cut the beets into bite-size chunks, and place them in a bowl.

2 While the beets are roasting, place the hazelnuts on another rimmed baking sheet and place them in the oven. Roast until they are toasted and fragrant, 10 to 15 minutes. Remove from the oven, let cool slightly, then rub off their skins and roughly chop the hazelnuts.

3 In a small bowl, whisk together the olive oil, balsamic, Dijon, salt, and pepper. Pour this dressing over the beets, toss to coat, then add the parsley, hazelnuts, and pomegranate seeds. Fold to combine.

SIDES ME UP! All of these salads would be delicious in a wrap or pita bread, or on top of cooked grains like brown rice or quinoa, for a complete meal.

ROLLOVER Roast extra beets to make the Polenta with Beet Ribbons and Arugula Pesto (page 141).

1.7 pounds / 750g beets

⅓ cup / 55g raw, unsalted hazelnuts

1½ teaspoons cold-pressed olive oil

1½ teaspoons balsamic vinegar

1½ teaspoons Dijon mustard

2 pinches of fine sea salt

Freshly ground black pepper

½ packed cup / 15g chopped fresh flat-leaf parsley

1 cup / 90g pomegranate seeds (from about 1 pomegranate)

ROASTED RADISHES AND AVOCADO

with Sesame Salt

Although enjoying radishes raw is definitely the norm, I'm all about cooking them for a seriously surprising change of pace. I can't believe just how different and tasty these rose-hued roots become with a little heat! Here I've roasted them, dialing down their distinctive bite; this allows their sweetness to shine through. Paired with creamy avocado, bright lemon, and Sesame Salt, this is a simple little side dish that would be a delicious way to start a meal.

SERVES 3 TO 4 ———————————————————————

15 to 20 radishes

1 tablespoon coconut oil, melted

1 large ripe avocado

Juice of 1 lemon

Handful of fresh chives, minced

Sesame Salt, for serving (recipe follows)

SIDES ME UP! To make this a meal, serve this salad over cooked brown rice, topped with crunchy sprouts.

1 Preheat the oven to 400°F / 200°C. Slice the radishes in half, place them on a rimmed baking sheet, and toss with the coconut oil. Roast until the radishes are tender and blistered in places, about 20 minutes. Remove them from the oven and let cool slightly.

2 Pit and peel the avocado, and then cut the flesh into cubes, about half the size of the radishes. Evenly divide the avocado cubes among individual plates, repeat with the radishes, and then pour half the lemon juice over the vegetables, adding more if desired. Sprinkle the chives and Sesame Salt over the top.

SESAME SALT

MAKES APPROXIMATELY ½ CUP / 75G

½ cup / 75g raw, unsalted sesame seeds

1½ teaspoons fine sea salt

In a large dry skillet, toast the sesame seeds over medium heat, stirring occasionally, until fragrant, 2 to 3 minutes, being careful not to burn them. Remove from the heat and transfer the seeds to a food processor or mortar. Add the salt and process until about half the seeds are broken. The mixture will keep in an airtight jar at room temperature for up to 2 months.

KALE, MUSHROOMS, AND WALNUTS

with Pecorino

⅓ cup / 35g raw, unsalted walnuts

1 small yellow onion

2 garlic cloves

½ pound / 250g cremini mushrooms

1½ teaspoons coconut oil or ghee

Fine sea salt

½ teaspoon dried thyme

2 cups / 60g chopped kale

1 tablespoon balsamic vinegar

Freshly ground black pepper

1 tablespoon cold-pressed olive oil (optional)

Freshly grated Pecorino Romano or Parmesan, for serving

ROLLOVER Caramelize extra onions for the Portobello Pizzas (page 119).

This little plate is like a walk in the autumn forest: deep, dark, and earthy. Grounding mushrooms and greens get a lift from sweet-and-sour vinegar notes and a light dusting of salty cheese. The walnuts add a particularly pleasing crunch, but almonds or pecans would be equally tasty.

SERVES 2 TO 3 ——————————————————————

1 Preheat a dry skillet over medium heat. When hot, toast the walnuts until fragrant and just golden, 3 to 4 minutes. Remove the pan from the heat, let the nuts cool, then roughly chop them.

2 Prepare the vegetables: Slice the onion into thin rounds, mince the garlic, and quarter the mushrooms.

3 Wipe the skillet clean of any walnut skins, then melt 1 teaspoon of the coconut oil over medium-high heat. Add the onion and a pinch of sea salt and stir to coat. Cook, stirring occasionally, until the onions soften and are nicely caramelized, at least 15 minutes. Remove the onions from the pan and set them aside.

4 Without cleaning the skillet, melt the remaining ghee and add the mushrooms. Let cook without stirring until the mushrooms brown on one side, at least 5 minutes. (They will seem dry at first, but they will release their water as they cook.) Give them a shake, and cook for a few minutes more without disturbing them. When the mushrooms are soft and juicy, add the thyme and garlic, and cook for 1 minute more. Add the kale and balsamic vinegar and remove from the heat just as the kale wilts and turns bright green, after about 2 minutes. Season with salt and black pepper. Fold in the caramelized onions, toasted walnuts, and olive oil.

5 To serve, place a small mound of the mixture on each plate (or add all of it to a serving platter) and grate the cheese over top. Enjoy warm.

SIDES ME UP! This meal makes an outstanding breakfast or lunch when topped with a soft-boiled egg.

GRILLED ASPARAGUS
with Lemony Goat Cheese Cream

Nothing says spring like those early shoots of green asparagus pushing through the thawing earth; they're also the first sign of life in the grocery store after months of winter. Asparagus is delicious both cooked and raw, and here I've lightly grilled the spears before setting them on a luscious bed of lemon-kissed goat cheese cream. This sauce pairs really well with roasted vegetables or even simple salad greens.

SERVES 3 TO 4

1 Heat a grill (or grill pan) to high. Snap off the tough ends of the asparagus where they naturally break. Coat each spear with just a little of the coconut oil.

2 Place the asparagus on the grill and let it cook on one side until it has charred slightly, about 5 minutes. Turn and cook for a few minutes more, until each piece is tender and nicely grilled.

3 Meanwhile, make the cream: Blend the goat cheese, garlic, lemon zest, olive oil, and lemon juice in a blender until completely smooth and creamy, adding 1 to 3 tablespoons of water to thin the sauce, as desired. Season with salt.

4 To serve, place a pool of sauce on each plate, then arrange the desired number of asparagus spears on top. Drizzle with extra olive oil if desired and season liberally with salt.

SIDES ME UP! Place the asparagus over cooked wild rice and lentils, top with toasted pistachios, and drizzle with the Lemony Goat Cheese Cream.

ROLLOVER Make double the Lemony Goat Cheese Cream to serve with Terrific Tarragon Green Bean Salad (page 68).

ASPARAGUS

1 pound / 450g (1 bunch) asparagus

1 teaspoon coconut oil or ghee

Cold-pressed olive oil for serving (optional)

Fine sea salt

LEMONY GOAT CHEESE CREAM

3½ ounces / 100g soft goat cheese

1 small garlic clove, finely minced

Zest of 1 lemon

1½ teaspoons cold-pressed olive oil

1 tablespoon freshly squeezed lemon juice

Fine sea salt

BROWN BUTTER CARROTS
with Pistachios and Dill

If you're still not convinced that simple food can be wildly delicious, give this recipe a try. With just a few humble ingredients, you can have a truly gourmet food experience!

Brown butter is made by cooking butter until the milk solids in it have caramelized, creating a richer, deeper, nutty-flavored butter. If you cannot find young carrots (look for them in the spring and early summer), use regular large carrots and slice them in half lengthwise before roasting. This will also help reduce the cooking time.

SERVES 2

1 Preheat the oven to 400°F / 200°C. Scrub the carrots well (do not peel them), and trim off all but 1 inch / 2.5cm of the tops. Rub each carrot with a little coconut oil and place them on a rimmed baking sheet. Season with salt and roast until the carrots are tender and blistered, 20 to 30 minutes.

2 Meanwhile, make the dressing: In a small skillet, melt the butter over medium heat. Add the shallot and swirl the pan over the heat until the butter has changed color from yellow to light brown, 5 to 7 minutes (the butter can burn very quickly, so keep an eye on it). Remove from the heat and pour the butter and shallot mixture into a jar with the mustard, vinegar, and a generous pinch of salt. Seal the jar and shake vigorously to blend.

3 Remove the carrots from the oven and place them on a platter. Pour the dressing over top and scatter the pistachios and dill over top. Serve immediately (the dressing will harden if left at room temperature for too long).

SIDES ME UP! Turn this into a complete meal by serving the carrots over cooked green lentils.

14 young carrots with tops

2 teaspoons coconut oil or ghee

Fine sea salt

2 tablespoons unsalted butter

1 shallot, finely diced

½ teaspoon Dijon mustard

1½ teaspoons apple cider vinegar

1 tablespoon raw, unsalted pistachios, lightly toasted and chopped

Handful of fresh dill

ROLLOVER Roast twice as many carrots to make the Wild Rice, Roasted Carrot, and Pomegranate Bold Bowl (page 147).

MARINATED ROASTED RED PEPPERS

with Chickpeas

4 large red bell peppers, stems, seeds, and ribs removed

1½ teaspoons coconut oil

3 tablespoons cold-pressed olive oil

2 tablespoons balsamic vinegar

2 pinches of fine sea salt

¼ teaspoon freshly ground black pepper

3 tablespoons raisins

Handful of fresh, flat-leaf parsley leaves

1½ cups / 225g (1 15-oz. can) cooked chickpeas, drained and rinsed

3½ ounces / 100g feta (preferably goat or sheep)

ROLLOVER Roast double the amount of red peppers and make Romesco Sauce (page 195).

Something really magical happens when you roast bell peppers. They turn from rather uptight, rigid (though tasty) fruits to silky smooth, relaxed, languid things that beg to mingle with complementary tastes. In this dish I've combined the sweet peppers with salty feta, bright parsley, and tender chickpeas. With a quick soak in a balsamic bath, the flavors of these ingredients become incredibly rich and satisfying for such a small dish.

SERVES 4 ——————————————

1 Preheat the oven to 400°F / 200°C. Rub the peppers with the coconut oil and place them on a rimmed baking sheet lined with foil. Roast until blistered and blackened in a few places, 35 to 40 minutes. Remove the peppers from the baking sheet, place them in a bowl, and quickly cover it with plastic wrap to steam the peppers, which makes the skin very easy to remove. When the peppers are cool enough to handle, remove and discard the skins.

2 While the peppers are roasting, in a medium bowl, whisk together the olive oil, vinegar, salt, and pepper. Mince the raisins and chop the parsley.

3 Tear or slice the skinned roasted peppers into large pieces and place them in the bowl with the dressing. Add the chickpeas, toss to coat, and let marinate for about 15 minutes.

4 Divide the mixture evenly among 4 plates. Sprinkle with the minced raisins and parsley and crumble the feta over top. Serve immediately.

SIDES ME UP! Make this a main dish by serving it over cooked quinoa.

CHARRED EGGPLANT BABA GANOUSH

with Pine Nuts

The secret to really good baba ganoush is charring the heck out of the eggplant skin. After years of roasting the eggplants in the oven for this dish, I've finally cracked the code by firing up my gas stove. This process delivers an unmistakable smoky depth and dimension to the dip that you just can't achieve any other way. It's kind of a messy process but worth every piece of ash left behind. Serve this with whole-grain pita bread or raw sticks of veggies, or tuck it into a lettuce wrap.

MAKES 2 CUPS / 500ML ─────────────────────────────

1 Prick the eggplants all over with a fork to help the steam escape when they are roasting. Turn three separate gas burners to medium and place the eggplants directly on top of the flames (alternatively, you can do this under a broiler or on an outdoor grill). Let cook, using tongs to turn each one frequently so that they char evenly, until the eggplants are completely soft and blackened, 15 to 20 minutes. Let them cool slightly, then cut each one lengthwise down the middle and scoop out the flesh into a bowl, discarding any burnt pieces.

2 In a food processor, pulse the garlic until minced. Add the eggplant flesh, olive oil, salt, and lemon juice, and blend until smooth and creamy. Place the baba ganoush in a medium bowl and season with more salt, as desired.

3 Preheat a dry skillet over medium heat. When hot, toast the pine nuts until slightly golden, 2 to 3 minutes. Immediately remove the pan from the heat and sprinkle the nuts over the baba ganoush. Garnish with chopped parsley, if desired, followed by a generous drizzle of olive oil.

3 medium eggplants

1 garlic clove

¼ cup cold-pressed olive oil, plus more for serving

¼ teaspoon fine sea salt, plus more as needed

2 teaspoons freshly squeezed lemon juice

2 tablespoons / 25g raw, unsalted pine nuts

Small handful of fresh flat-leaf parsley leaves, for garnish (optional)

SIDES ME UP! Make this a meal by spreading the creamy baba ganoush onto 2 slices of whole-grain bread or pita with sliced red peppers, crumbled feta, and arugula.

BAKED FETA

with Olives, Peppers, and Tomatoes

1 cup / 100g cherry tomatoes

½ red bell pepper, stem, seeds, and ribs removed

⅓ cup / 60g kalamata olives

2 teaspoons dried oregano

Pinch each of sea salt and freshly ground black pepper

7 ounces / 200g block feta (preferably goat or sheep)

Cold-pressed olive oil, for drizzling

Small handful of fresh flat-leaf parsley leaves, for garnish

Crusty whole-grain bread or pita, for serving (optional)

Until I discovered this concept, I'd only ever tried feta cold in salads or as part of a mezze platter. But *this* is the new hotness. Baked feta is a revelation, especially when smothered with juicy veggies, herbs, and olives. It makes the most wonderful starter to a meal, or it could even be served on the side of a large green salad for a weekend lunch. I like drizzling it generously with olive oil and pairing it with crusty bread to soak up all the delectable juices. However simple, this is definitely one of my favorite recipes in the whole book.

SERVES 2 TO 4

1 Preheat the oven to 400°F / 200°C.

2 Slice the tomatoes into quarters. Cut the pepper into similarly sized pieces. Pit the olives and roughly chop them. Place everything in a bowl and toss with the oregano, salt, and pepper.

3 Place the feta in an ovenproof dish. Top with the vegetable mixture and bake until the vegetables are roasted and the cheese is soft, 20 to 25 minutes. Just before serving, drizzle with olive oil and sprinkle with parsley. Enjoy the baked cheese right out of the oven with crusty whole-grain bread or pita.

SIDES ME UP! Wrap half the block of the feta and the vegetables with a large leaf of romaine lettuce (or a whole-grain wrap), add fresh sprouts, and enjoy.

BROCCOLI

with Garlic Ghee and Pine Nuts

We all need to eat more broccoli. Thankfully, this recipe can definitely help in that department. I could sit down and eat an entire bowl of this for dinner—it's *that* tasty. It's also super simple, easy to make, and comes together in a matter of minutes, so you have no excuse for not eating more of this protein-rich, phytonutrient all-star.

Remember that ghee is made with unsalted butter, so this dish will need extra seasoning right at the end. I like to hit it with plenty of good flaky sea salt just after pouring the ghee over so that it sticks to the florets. You can use salted butter in a pinch, but cut back on salting the finished dish if you do. To change things up, use cashews instead of the pine nuts.

1 large head of broccoli

2 tablespoons / 25g raw, unsalted pine nuts

2 tablespoons ghee

2 garlic cloves, minced

Plenty of flaky sea salt

SIDES ME UP! Make this a main dish by serving the broccoli over whole-grain noodles or pasta.

ROLLOVER Steam double the amount of broccoli for Broccoli Basil Broth with Noodles and Sesame Salt (page 40).

SERVES 4 ——————————————————————————

1 Wash the broccoli and cut it into equal-size florets, including the long stem (just trim off the bottom).

2 In a large pot fitted with a steamer basket, bring a small amount of water to a boil. Add the broccoli, cover, and steam until tender-crisp, about 5 to 7 minutes depending on the size of the florets, being careful not to overcook. Place the broccoli on a serving platter.

3 While the broccoli is cooking, preheat a dry skillet over medium heat. When hot, toast the pine nuts until slightly golden, about 3 minutes. Transfer them to a dish and set aside to cool.

4 In the same skillet, melt the ghee. Add the minced garlic and fry just until one or two of the pieces starts to turn golden, about 1 minute. Immediately remove from the heat, pour the garlic oil over the broccoli, and toss to coat. Scatter the pine nuts on top and sprinkle with salt. Serve warm.

GRILLED SPRING ONIONS

with Lemon-Marinated Chickpeas

1½ cups / 225g (1 15-oz. can) cooked chickpeas, drained and rinsed

Zest and juice of 1 lemon

Pinch each of fine sea salt and freshly ground black pepper, plus more as needed

1 tablespoon cold-pressed olive oil, plus more for serving

16 spring onions

2 teaspoons coconut oil

Flaky sea salt, for serving

Beans are great for marinating because they are wonderful blank canvases for flavor and willingly absorb anything you anoint them with. Here, a simple mixture of lemon, olive oil, and black pepper transforms the humble chickpea into a super-tasty base for smoky grilled spring onions—a match made in heaven!

SERVES 2 TO 3 ————————————————————

1 In a medium bowl, combine the chickpeas, lemon zest and juice, salt, pepper, and olive oil. Stir to coat, cover, and let the chickpeas marinate at room temperature for at least 15 minutes, or up to 24 hours in the fridge (the longer the better!).

2 Heat a grill (or grill pan) to high. Wash and slice off the very tops of the spring onions. Lightly rub the onions with the coconut oil and place them on the grill. Cook, turning once or twice, until the onions are tender and slightly charred, 7 to 10 minutes.

3 Taste the chickpeas and adjust the seasonings, as desired. Place them on a large plate or platter and lay the grilled onions on top. Spoon any extra marinade over the top, drizzle with olive oil, and sprinkle with flaky sea salt.

SIDES ME UP! Turn this into a more substantial dish with cooked quinoa and some toasted almonds.

ROLLOVER Marinate extra chickpeas to use in the Rainbow Hummus Bowl (page 74).

COPYCAT COUSCOUS

with Clementines

Celeriac, sometimes referred to as celery root, is one aggressive-looking vegetable, with an appearance that is sure to intimidate just about anyone who isn't familiar with its surprisingly gentle flavor. With a taste similar to celery stalks, but far milder and sweetly nutty, celeriac is incredibly versatile and delicious in many applications. Here I've minced it in the food processor to make something that resembles couscous, then mixed it with clementines, pumpkin seeds, and parsley. This is a simple, delicious, and fresh little salad or side dish for the cooler months.

SERVES 3 TO 4

5 cups / 750g peeled and roughly chopped celeriac (about 1 large celeriac)

½ teaspoon fine sea salt, plus more as needed

1 tablespoon freshly squeezed lemon juice

2 tablespoons cold-pressed olive oil

⅓ cup / 50g raw, unsalted pumpkin seeds

1 cup / 120g sliced green olives

1 packed cup / 30g fresh flat-leaf parsley leaves

2 clementines (tangerines or mandarins will also work), segmented and cut into small chunks

1 shallot, diced

1 In a food processor, pulse the celeriac with the sea salt and lemon juice until it is finely minced. Transfer to a large serving bowl and toss with the olive oil.

2 Preheat a dry skillet over medium heat. When hot, toast the pumpkin seeds, tossing often, until fragrant, 4 to 5 minutes. Remove the pan from the heat and set aside.

3 Add the green olives, parsley, clementines, shallot, and pumpkin seeds to the bowl with the celeriac. Toss all of the ingredients together and season with salt.

SIDES ME UP! To make this a meal, add some cooked chickpeas or lentils and a drizzle of Minty Tahini Dressing (page 63).

ROLLOVER Double the celeriac couscous and use it instead of bulgur in the Ceremonial Stuffed Pumpkin with Bulgur, Feta, and Figs (page 143).

TWINKLE, TWINKLE, JEWELED RICE

2 small yellow onions or 4 shallots

2 medium carrots

1 orange

Knob of coconut oil or ghee

1½ teaspoons cumin seeds

1 teaspoon ground turmeric

4 bay leaves

4 green cardamom pods, crushed

1 cinnamon stick

½ cup / 75g mixed dried fruit (dates, apricots, raisins, cranberries)

2 cups / 400g brown basmati rice, rinsed (if you can, soak the rice for up to 8 hours)

1 teaspoon fine sea salt, plus more as needed

½ cup / 70g raw, unsalted almonds

½ packed cup / 12g chopped fresh mint leaves

½ packed cup / 11g chopped fresh chives

1 cup / 90g pomegranate seeds (from about 1 pomegranate)

Cold-pressed olive oil, for drizzling

1 lemon, cut into wedges, for serving

This golden, glistening, gem-colored rice dish is inspired by a classic Iranian recipe that features warm, fragrant spices, dried fruits, and nuts—and is a true labor of love to make! I've simplified the process by cooking everything together in one pot, and I've made it healthier by replacing white rice with brown. Although the lemon added at the end may seem like an afterthought, it is an essential element of the dish, rounding out the flavors and adding a zesty kick.

SERVES 8

1 Dice the onions and grate the carrots.

2 Using a vegetable peeler or a small sharp knife, peel the rind from the orange, removing as little white pith as possible. Slice the rind into matchstick-size strips and set aside. Reserve the orange flesh for another use.

3 In a medium pot, melt the coconut oil over medium heat. Add the cumin seeds and cook until fragrant, 1 minute, then add the turmeric, bay leaves, cardamom pods, and the cinnamon stick. Stir to coat with the oil and fry for another minute until fragrant. Next, add the onions, carrots, orange zest, and dried fruit. Cook until the onion softens, about 5 minutes.

4 Drain the rice and add it to the pot with 4 cups / 1 liter of water and the salt. Cover the pot, bring the liquid to a boil, then reduce the heat to low and cook until the water has evaporated, about 45 minutes.

5 Roast the almonds: Preheat the oven to 300°F / 150°C. Spread the almonds on a rimmed baking sheet in a single layer and roast until they are fragrant and slightly darker in color, 20 to 25 minutes. (A good way to check is to bite one in half and check the color in the center—it should

be golden.) Remove from the oven and let cool completely. Roughly chop the almonds.

6 When the rice is finished cooking, remove from the heat. Scoop the rice out onto a large serving platter to cool slightly and to prevent the grains from sticking together. Sprinkle with the herbs, almonds, and pomegranate seeds. Fold to incorporate. Taste and adjust the seasoning (you will likely need to add more salt at this stage). Squeeze a few of the lemon wedges over top.

7 Serve the rice with a drizzle of olive oil and more lemon wedges.

SIDES ME UP! This is delicious with sautéed eggplant or mushrooms, a poached egg, and cooked lentils or chickpeas.

CHARRED CABBAGE
with Apples and Toasted Walnut Sauce

Like grilling, charring lends a complexity to underrated veggies like cabbage. Humble, mild foods take on a whole new taste and texture. The trick is not overdoing it—you want to caramelize them, not burn them! I like pairing charred veggies with something rich and creamy, like this Toasted Walnut Sauce. The fresh, diced apples complete this dish with their acidic high note and crunch.

SERVES 3 TO 6

1 Remove the outer leaves from the cabbage. Cut the cabbage into 6 wedges, leaving the base stem intact so that the leaves stay together.

2 In a large skillet, bring ½ cup / 125ml of water to a simmer, add the salt, and stir to dissolve. Lay the cabbage wedges in the simmering water, cover, and steam them until tender, about 5 minutes (the time may vary slightly, depending on the size of your cabbage). Remove the lid, place the cabbage on a plate, and discard the water from the skillet.

3 Put the skillet back on the stove and melt the coconut oil over high heat. When the oil is hot, put the cabbage back in the skillet and cook, uncovered and undisturbed, until a good char has developed, about 5 minutes (again, the time may vary slightly, depending on the size of your cabbage). Turn the wedges to brown them on their other sides for 5 minutes more.

4 While the cabbage is cooking, dice the apple into very small cubes. In a small bowl, toss the apple with the lemon juice. Finely mince a few parsley leaves and combine them with the apple.

5 To serve, place 1 or 2 cabbage wedges on each plate, add the apple, drizzle the Toasted Walnut Sauce over top, and garnish with flaky sea salt and extra parsley.

1 small head white cabbage

¼ teaspoon fine sea salt

1½ teaspoons coconut oil or ghee

1 large apple

1 teaspoon freshly squeezed lemon juice

Small handful of fresh flat-leaf parsley leaves

Toasted Walnut Sauce, for serving (page 84)

Flaky sea salt, for garnish

SIDES ME UP! Make this a main dish by serving it over cooked wild rice.

ROLLOVER Double the Toasted Walnut Sauce to use the extra on the Arugula and Fig Salad with Toasted Walnut Sauce (page 82).

ROASTED BRUSSELS SPROUTS

with Maple Walnuts

MAPLE WALNUTS

¾ cup / 75g raw, unsalted walnuts

1 tablespoon pure maple syrup

2 pinches of flaky sea salt

BRUSSELS SPROUTS

1 pound / 500g Brussels sprouts

1½ teaspoons coconut oil or ghee, melted

Maple-Mustard Dressing, for serving (page 69)

2 pinches of fine sea salt, to taste

Freshly ground black pepper

⅓ cup / 30g pomegranate seeds

ROLLOVER Use the extra pomegranate seeds for the Wild Rice, Roasted Carrot, and Pomegranate Bold Bowl (page 147). Make extra Maple Walnuts to top the Brilliant Banana Almond Soft-Serve (page 221).

It still amazes me how the simplest things can also be the most complex tasting and delicious. This dish is a prime example of that. Roasted Brussels sprouts combine beautifully with the bright tang of pomegranates and the toasty, caramelized sweetness of Maple Walnuts, which will be your new go-to topping for all manner of roasted veggies and hearty green salads too. There is something so satisfying about chopping them up—shards of condensed syrup crackling under the blade of your knife. You can make them two days in advance to save yourself some time.

SERVES 3 TO 4

1 Prepare the walnuts: Preheat the oven to 350°F / 180°C. Place the walnuts on a rimmed baking sheet with the maple syrup and salt. Toss to coat and bake for 7 to 10 minutes, tossing once after 5 minutes when the walnuts begin to bubble. Remove from the oven and let cool completely.

2 Meanwhile, roast the Brussels sprouts: Remove any damaged outer leaves from the Brussels sprouts and slice the sprouts in half lengthwise. Place them on a rimmed baking sheet and toss with the coconut oil to coat. Roast until the sprouts are tender but not overcooked, about 15 minutes.

3 While the sprouts are roasting, roughly chop the cooled walnuts.

4 When the Brussels sprouts are cooked through, remove them from the oven and immediately drizzle them with the Maple-Mustard Dressing, toss to coat, and season with salt and pepper. Place them in a large bowl or serving platter, then scatter the pomegranate seeds and Maple Walnuts on top. Serve warm.

SIDES ME UP! This dish works really well for dinner when served over cooked lentils.

SO-SIMPLE ROASTED ROOTS
with Dukkah

2 pounds / 1kg mixed root vegetables, such as sweet potato, carrot, beet, parsnip, rutabaga, turnip, and onion

1 tablespoon coconut oil or ghee

Fine sea salt and freshly ground black pepper

Garnishes of your choice, such as lemon zest, crushed red pepper flakes, and fresh herbs (parsley, cilantro, basil, mint, rosemary, thyme)

Dukkah, for serving (page 26)

It seems almost silly to write such an easy recipe, but in truth, roasted veggies form the foundation of so many of my favorite meals. Inexpensive, versatile, and practically foolproof to make, they are a great place to start when you want to add more plants to your diet. Try different combinations of vegetables and cut them in creative ways to keep things interesting.

If you're looking for a different party hors d'oeuvre, try serving these roasted veggies with Dukkah, an Egyptian nut and spice blend that is wildly delicious. I like to simply dip the veg in the Dukkah, which gives them a nutty, seasoned coating.

SERVES 4

1 Preheat the oven to 350°F / 180°C.

2 Peel any vegetables that require peeling (such as beets, rutabagas, and turnips). Cut the vegetables into similar-size pieces so that they cook evenly. Place on a rimmed baking sheet with the coconut oil and transfer the baking sheet to the oven.

3 Roast until the oil has melted, about 5 minutes, then remove from the oven and toss to coat. Place them back in the oven and roast until the vegetables are tender but not mushy, 25 to 30 minutes.

4 Remove from the oven, season the vegetables generously with sea salt and pepper, and garnish with fresh herbs, citrus zest, and pepper flakes, if desired. Serve with Dukkah. Store leftovers in an airtight container in the fridge for 3 to 4 days.

ROLLOVER Make extra roasted roots, store them in the fridge, and use them to top soups and salads, fold them into cooked whole grains, or blend them up with beans for a dip, such as Roasted Beet and Caper Hummus (page 189).

SIDES ME UP! Roasted veggies can easily turn into a meal simply by adding cooked quinoa or brown rice, black beans or chickpeas, and a poached egg.

SNACKS

SAVORY

HUMMUS, 3 WAYS   187

STONE FRUIT GINGER SALSA
WITH BAKED CORN CHIPS   191

CHARRED GREEN BEANS WITH ROMESCO SAUCE   193

SIMPLE MINT PEA DIP   196

SPICY FRICOS   199

ROASTED SESAME AVOCADO CREAM   200

QUINOA CORN MUFFINS   203

LOGIC-DEFYING ZUCCHINI FRIES   204

CARROT CUMIN FIRECRACKERS   207

SOUR CREAM & ONION CHICKPEA CRISPS   209

SPICY-SWEET PUMPKIN SEED SNACKS   211

SWEET

SUNBUTTER RYE TOASTS WITH
SALTED MAPLE STRAWBERRIES   212

SWEET POTATO DATE MUFFINS   214

SPICY WATERMELON MOJITO ICE POPS   217

HONEY ALMOND GRANOLA BARS   218

BRILLIANT BANANA ALMOND SOFT-SERVE   221

COCONUT CARDAMOM BLUEBERRY
SNACK CAKE   222

TOASTED WALNUT BROWNIE BITES, 3 WAYS   224

DOUBLE CHOCOLATE CHUNK
SUNBUTTER COOKIES   228

PREVIOUS PAGE, from left to right: Smoky Roasted Carrot Hummus, page 188 /
Roasted Beet and Caper Hummus, page 189 / Superb Herb Hummus, page 188

HUMMUS, 3 WAYS

Need to shake up your hummus game? Try these winners on for size! We'll start with the basic recipe and then add herbs, spices, and roasted veggies to the mix for three surprising twists on the classic: Smoky Roasted Carrot Hummus, Superb Herb Hummus, and Roasted Beet and Caper Hummus.

You will have to add salt to suit your taste in these recipes, as salt amounts will vary greatly if you are using canned chickpeas and store-bought tahini. Start off with a few pinches and work up from there, tasting as you go.

ROLLOVER Use any of these variations in the Rainbow Hummus Bowl (page 74), and all of them are delicious served with the Carrot Cumin Firecrackers (page 207).

BASIC HUMMUS

SERVES 4 ————————————————————————

1 In a food processor, pulse the garlic until it is finely minced.

2 Add the tahini, cumin, lemon zest and juice, and olive oil, and purée to make a paste.

3 Add the chickpeas, pulse, and add up to ¼ cup / 60ml of water to thin as needed until the desired consistency is reached. Season with salt.

4 Store the hummus in an airtight container in the fridge for up to 5 days.

1 garlic clove

¼ cup / 60ml tahini

1 teaspoon ground cumin

Zest of 1 lemon

3 tablespoons freshly squeezed lemon juice

2 tablespoons cold-pressed olive oil

1½ cups / 225g (1 15-oz. can) cooked chickpeas, drained and rinsed

Fine sea salt

SMOKY ROASTED CARROT HUMMUS

3 large carrots

1 teaspoon coconut oil

Basic Hummus (page 187)

½ teaspoon smoked hot paprika (ground chipotle would also work)

Pinch of cayenne pepper (optional)

1 tablespoon freshly squeezed lemon juice

Fine sea salt

SERVES 4

1 Preheat the oven to 400°F / 200°C. Scrub the carrots well and slice them in half lengthwise. Rub each carrot with a little of the coconut oil and place them on a rimmed baking sheet.

2 Roast the carrots until they are tender and blistered but not overcooked, 15 to 20 minutes.

3 Remove the carrots from the oven and place them in a food processor with the hummus, paprika, cayenne, and lemon juice. Purée until smooth. Season with salt.

SUPERB HERB HUMMUS

Basic Hummus (page 187)

1½ teaspoons freshly squeezed lemon juice

1 tablespoon cold-pressed olive oil

1½ teaspoons pure maple syrup

½ cup / 14g each chopped fresh chives, mint, cilantro, and flat-leaf parsley

Fine sea salt

SERVES 4

In a food processor, combine the Basic Hummus, lemon juice, olive oil, maple syrup, and herbs. Purée until the desired consistency is reached. Season with salt.

ROASTED BEET AND CAPER HUMMUS

SERVES 4 ————————————————————————

1 Preheat the oven to 400°F / 200°C. Wrap the beets individually in foil and place them on a rimmed baking sheet. Roast for about 30 minutes. The beets are ready when you can insert a sharp knife into the center without too much resistance—they should be tender, not mushy. Remove the beets from the oven, peel back the foil a little, and let them cool. When the beets are cool enough to handle, peel off and discard the skins, then cut the beets into quarters.

2 In a food processor, combine the beets, hummus, capers, and lemon juice. Purée until the desired consistency is reached. Season with salt.

3 small beets

Basic Hummus (page 187)

3 tablespoons capers, drained

1 tablespoon freshly squeezed lemon juice

Fine sea salt

STONE FRUIT GINGER SALSA
with Baked Corn Chips

When I began working on an organic farm in Northern California, I arrived at the peak of harvest season. But instead of being out in the garden picking fruits and veggies, my job was to process everything that came into the kitchen. At first this seemed like a total blessing, but it became a huge challenge to figure out ways to preserve the abundance of produce so it would last through the winter. After making a few peach pies and tarts for the freezer, I was pretty stumped on what to do with the remaining kilos of fruit. I am not sure how I came up with the idea, but "salsa" struck me like lightning, and I became the *queen* of peach salsa.

I tried to re-create the recipe I used back on the farm here, with the addition of fresh ginger, which really makes this something special. If you're into canning, this is a great salsa to make in big batches and preserve. Serve it as a snack with corn chips or alongside grilled vegetables with your main dish.

SERVES 4 ————————————————————

6 medium stone fruits, such as peaches, nectarines, or apricots

1 small red chile (stem and seeds removed), minced (serrano is a good choice)

1 small red bell pepper (stem, seeds, and ribs removed), diced

1 tablespoon minced shallot or red onion

1½ teaspoons peeled, minced fresh ginger

⅓ packed cup / 15g chopped fresh cilantro leaves and tender stems

1½ teaspoons freshly squeezed lime juice

¼ teaspoon flaky sea salt

Baked Corn Chips (recipe follows), for serving (optional)

1 Wash, pit, and dice the stone fruits into very small pieces, then transfer them to a large bowl.

2 Add the chile, bell pepper, shallot, ginger, cilantro, lime juice, and salt. Taste and adjust the seasoning as needed, and let the salsa stand at room temperature, to allow the flavors to meld, at least 20 minutes.

3 Serve with Baked Corn Chips (recipe follows) or your favorite corn chips. The salsa does not keep well (unless you can it!), so be sure to eat it within 1 day.

ROLLOVER Make a double batch and use it in place of the Radish Cilantro Salsa for Quinoa and Black Beans with Radish Cilantro Salsa (page 106).

(recipe continues)

8 good-quality corn tortillas

2 to 3 tablespoons coconut oil, melted

Fine sea salt

BAKED CORN CHIPS

SERVES 4 TO 6

1 Preheat the oven to 350°F / 180°C.

2 Brush each tortilla round lightly with melted coconut oil on both sides, making sure to cover the edges as well. Sprinkle with salt.

3 Stack the tortillas on top of one another. Cut the stack into eighths. Place the triangular wedges on a rimmed baking sheet, overlapping as little as possible. Bake until the chips are crisp and just turning golden around the edges, 8 to 12 minutes; they will likely curl up a little on the baking sheet. The chips will continue to crisp up once removed from the oven. When they are completely cool, transfer them to an airtight container. Note that baked chips will become stale much faster than fried ones, so they are best consumed within a couple days.

CHARRED GREEN BEANS

with Romesco Sauce

1 pound / 500g green beans

1 tablespoon coconut oil, melted

Fine sea salt

Romesco Sauce (recipe follows)

Romesco is an intensely delicious sauce from the northeastern region of Spain, where fisherman typically serve it alongside whitefish, but it's delicious with grilled and roasted vegetables, eggs, and cooked grains, and it can even be thinned out a little to make a dressing for salad greens. Made with roasted red peppers, almonds, tomato paste, garlic, and smoked paprika, it hits all the umami notes, making the sauce satisfying, which is not typical of a simple vegetarian dish. I love pairing it with charred green beans; it's like a far more sophisticated and healthy version of fries and ketchup that kids will love.

SERVES 4

1 Preheat your grill (or grill pan) to high.

2 Wash and trim the green beans. Lightly coat them in the coconut oil and place on the grill. Cook for 4 to 5 minutes, then turn and cook until tender and nicely charred, 2 to 3 minutes more.

3 Remove the beans from the heat and season with salt. Serve with Romesco Sauce.

(recipe continues)

ROMESCO SAUCE

MAKES 1½ CUPS / 375ML

1 Preheat the oven to 400°F / 200°C.

2 Wash the bell peppers and cut them in half. Remove the stems, seeds, and ribs, and coat the pieces lightly with coconut oil. Place on a rimmed baking sheet and roast until blistered and blackened in a few places, 25 to 35 minutes. Remove the roasted peppers from the baking sheet, place them in a bowl, and quickly cover it with plastic wrap to steam the peppers, which makes the skin very easy to remove. When they are cool enough to handle, peel the peppers and discard the skins.

3 Reduce the oven temperature to 325°F / 160°C. Place the almonds on a separate rimmed baking sheet and toast for 10 to 12 minutes, watching them carefully so that they do not burn. Remove from the oven and set them aside to cool.

4 In a food processor, pulse the garlic until minced. Add the roasted peppers, almonds, paprika, olive oil, salt, parsley, tomato paste, and lemon juice and process until the desired consistency is reached—from slightly chunky to smooth. Season with salt.

4 medium red bell peppers

Coconut oil

½ cup / 70g raw, unsalted almonds

1 garlic clove

1 teaspoon smoked hot paprika (ground chipotle would also work)

2 tablespoons cold-pressed olive oil

¼ teaspoon fine sea salt, plus more as needed

3 tablespoons chopped fresh flat-leaf parsley

2 tablespoons tomato paste

1 teaspoon freshly squeezed lemon juice

SIMPLE MINT PEA DIP

(V) (GF) (GrF)

16 ounces / 500g fresh or frozen green peas

⅓ packed cup / 7g fresh mint leaves

1 large garlic clove

2 tablespoons tahini

¼ cup / 60ml freshly squeezed lemon juice

2 tablespoons cold-pressed olive oil

½ teaspoon fine sea salt

This recipe appeared on my blog some years back, but it's still the preferred snack in my house because it is fast and easy to make. It's both light and rich at the same time, and it pairs well with any spring or early summer veggies, crackers, or other "dippables." I even like to spread it on a large lettuce or cabbage leaf, wrap it up, and munch away. Peas and mint are a classic combo, and the lemon adds gorgeous brightness. Tahini, a slightly unusual addition, grounds everything in its satisfying nuttiness and makes the dip deliciously creamy. You can use fresh, raw peas for this recipe, but blanching them for just a couple of minutes brings out their delicate sweetness and enhances the overall flavor.

SERVES 4 TO 6 ——————————————————————

1 Fill a small saucepan with water and bring it to a boil. Add the peas and cook until they are bright green and sweet, 2 to 3 minutes, being careful not to overcook. Drain and rinse the peas under very cold water to halt the cooking process. Set aside.

2 Roughly chop the mint leaves. Set aside.

3 In a food processor, pulse the garlic until minced. Add the peas, mint, tahini, lemon juice, olive oil, and salt, and purée until smooth.

4 Store in an airtight container in the fridge for 3 to 4 days, but try to consume this dip as quickly as possible.

ROLLOVER Use this pea dip instead of hummus in the Rainbow Hummus Bowl (page 74).

SPICY FRICOS

Get your frico on! Fricos are small rounds of baked cheese that turn miraculously crunchy in the oven, and with just two ingredients, they are probably the simplest snack to make. Though they are typically prepared with Parmesan, in my version I use a hard sheep's milk cheese called Pecorino Romano, which is very similar. If you cannot find Pecorino at your grocery store, use Parmesan instead, but it's important that it comes in a wedge, not pre-grated. Fricos are very tasty served as a nibble before dinner with a crisp, sparkling beverage, or on top of a simple green salad. If you're not into spicy food, simply leave out the crushed red pepper flakes for a one-ingredient treat!

1 cup / 75g freshly grated Pecorino Romano

½ to 1 teaspoon crushed red pepper flakes (depending on how spicy you like them)

MAKES ABOUT 15 CHIPS

1 Preheat the oven to 325°F / 160°C.

2 In a medium bowl, combine the cheese and the pepper flakes, stirring to incorporate.

3 Line a rimmed baking sheet with parchment paper. Place heaping tablespoons of the grated cheese and pepper flake mixture about 1 inch / 2.5cm apart on the parchment paper and press down lightly with the bottom of a glass to flatten them slightly. Bake until golden, 8 to 10 minutes. Remove from the oven and let cool completely. Store leftovers in an airtight container at room temperature for up to 3 days.

ROLLOVER For extra crunch, use these instead of goat cheese in the Balsamic-Roasted Plums with Spinach and Goat Cheese (page 70).

ROASTED SESAME
AVOCADO CREAM

2 tablespoons raw, unsalted sesame seeds

1 garlic clove

Flesh of 2 ripe avocados

4 tablespoons freshly squeezed lime juice, plus more as desired

2 tablespoons tahini

¼ teaspoon pure maple syrup (optional)

Fine sea salt

½ packed cup / 20g fresh cilantro leaves

½ sheet of nori, sliced into very thin strips (optional)

Inspired by the Japanese flavor combination of avocado, sesame, and nori, I made an avocado dip full of surprises! The tahini adds a satisfying richness and complexity, while the toasted sesame seeds bring on the nuttiness and impart a wonderful contrast to the smooth creaminess. Serve this dip with vegetables or crackers, or use it in a sandwich or lettuce wrap instead of mayonnaise.

SERVES 4 ———————————————————————————

1 Preheat a dry skillet over medium heat. When hot, toast the sesame seeds, stirring often, until they are fragrant and beginning to pop, 2 to 3 minutes. Remove the pan from the heat and set aside.

2 In a food processor, pulse the garlic until minced.

3 Add the avocados, lime juice, tahini, maple syrup, salt, and cilantro. Purée until smooth and creamy. Taste and adjust the seasoning as needed. Fold in half of the sesame seeds and, if desired, the nori.

4 Spread the dip out on a large plate. Sprinkle with the remaining sesame seeds and, if desired, more nori strips. Serve immediately.

ROLLOVER This is a delicious dip to use with the So-Simple Roasted Roots with Dukkah (page 183).

QUINOA CORN MUFFINS

Growing up in the southern United States instilled in me a serious love of corn bread, but the high amounts of butter, cream, and sugar in classic versions negate most of the health benefits of the other ingredients. My recipe swaps white flour with corn flour, and sugar with maple syrup, and adds wonderful texture with cooked quinoa. The chile delivers a swift kick, and the cilantro adds tons of southwestern style. These muffins are delicious served alongside a steaming bowl of chili (page 138) or a black bean salad.

MAKES 12 MUFFINS

1 Preheat the oven to 400°F / 200°C. Line a cupcake pan with 12 muffin liners.

2 In a large bowl, sift together the cornmeal, corn flour, baking powder, baking soda, and salt. Add the cooked quinoa.

3 In a separate bowl, whisk together the milk, eggs, coconut oil, and maple syrup.

4 Add the wet ingredients to the dry and combine in as few strokes as possible. Fold in the cilantro and minced chile.

5 Spoon the batter into muffin cups until they are about three-quarters full and sprinkle evenly with the pumpkin seeds. Bake until the edges are golden brown and a toothpick comes out clean when inserted into the middle of a muffin, about 25 minutes. The muffins are best enjoyed fresh but will keep in an airtight container at room temperature for 3 to 4 days.

GF

1½ cups / 250g cornmeal

½ cup / 75g corn flour

1 tablespoon baking powder

½ teaspoon baking soda

1 teaspoon fine sea salt

1 cup / 140g cooked quinoa (from about ⅓ cup / 55g dry)

1 cup / 250ml plant-based milk of your choice

3 large eggs

⅓ cup / 80ml coconut oil, melted

1½ teaspoons pure maple syrup

½ cup / 15g chopped fresh cilantro leaves and tender stems

1 small red chile (stem and seeds removed), minced (serrano is a good choice)

3 tablespoons raw, unsalted pumpkin seeds

LOGIC-DEFYING
ZUCCHINI FRIES

1½ cups / 140g freshly grated Pecorino Romano (Parmesan will also work)

1 tablespoon garlic powder

1½ teaspoons freshly ground black pepper

½ teaspoon fine sea salt

2 teaspoons dried oregano

3 to 4 medium zucchini

1 tablespoon coconut oil or ghee, melted

Hot sauce, for serving (optional)

Is it nuts to suggest that you or anyone you know would eat an entire zucchini in one sitting? I wager that you'll actually be *fighting* over the last pieces of these totally surprising and, dare I say it, addictive nibbles! Even picky kids I know who claim not to like vegetables gobble them up and beg for more.

The base of cheese, salt, and pepper is lovely with the addition of oregano, but rosemary, thyme, or crushed red pepper flakes also make a tasty change-up. If your grocery store does not sell Pecorino cheese, a wedge of Parmesan will work.

SERVES 4

1 Preheat the oven to 350°F / 180°C. Set a wire rack inside a rimmed baking sheet.

2 In a medium bowl, combine the cheese, garlic powder, black pepper, salt, and oregano.

3 Slice the zucchini into thin wedges; you should get about 12 pieces from each vegetable. Toss the wedges in the coconut oil to coat, then toss them in the cheese mixture, pressing the wedges into the cheese to set. Place the coated fries on the wire rack.

4 Bake the zucchini fries until tender, 12 to 15 minutes, then place them under the broiler until the cheese is golden, 3 to 4 minutes. Serve immediately with hot sauce, if desired.

ROLLOVER Serve leftover fries with Romesco Sauce (page 195).

CARROT CUMIN FIRECRACKERS

These savory, spicy crisps are a simple and tasty way to shake up your boxed cracker routine. Never endeavored to bake crackers before? No worries—these are a cinch to make, and you probably have everything you need in your cupboard right now. The carrots, cumin seeds, and crushed red pepper flakes really do make these look like pyrotechnic treats, and the taste is simply explosive!

MAKES ABOUT 40 SMALL CRACKERS ─────────────────────────

1 In a small bowl, combine the flax seeds with 6 tablespoons / 90ml of the water. Set aside to gel, about 15 minutes. Meanwhile, in a food processor, pulse 2¾ cups / 275g of the oats until they resemble a rough flour. Add the spices and salt; pulse to incorporate.

2 Transfer the oat mixture to a large bowl. Add the coconut oil, flax seed gel, and the remaining 6 tablespoons / 90ml of water; stir to combine. Add the carrots and finish mixing.

3 Preheat the oven to 350°F / 180°C. Divide the dough in half and place one half on a large sheet of parchment paper and then set another sheet on top.

4 Using a rolling pin, roll out the dough into a very thin round or square. Remove the top layer of parchment and sprinkle 2 tablespoons of the remaining rolled oats on top, replace the parchment, and roll to set.

5 Remove the top piece of parchment paper and score the dough into the desired cracker shapes (squares, rectangles, triangles) using the tip of a sharp knife. Slide the dough and the parchment paper onto a rimmed baking sheet and place it in the oven.

6 Bake the crackers until fragrant and golden brown, 25 to 30 minutes. Repeat steps 4 through 6 with the remaining dough.

2 tablespoons flax seeds

12 tablespoons / 180ml water

3 cups / 300g gluten-free rolled oats

1 tablespoon cumin seeds

½ teaspoon crushed red pepper flakes

½ teaspoon ground chipotle or smoked hot paprika

1 teaspoon fine sea salt

3 tablespoons coconut oil, melted

1 medium carrot, grated

SOUR CREAM AND ONION CHICKPEA CRISPS

If you love sour cream 'n' onion chips, you will totally flip over these salty and super-crunchy chickpea crisps. Pack them in your kids' lunchboxes, too, or serve them at cocktail hour instead of nuts or chips. I always make a double batch so I have extra to garnish salads and soups with a great gluten-free, high-protein crouton replacement. Keep in mind that the chickpeas will crisp up quite a bit outside of the oven, so it's okay if they are still a little soft when they are finished roasting.

SERVES 4 TO 6

3 tablespoons coconut oil

1½ teaspoons freshly squeezed lemon juice

2 teaspoons dried dill

4 teaspoons onion powder

1 teaspoon fine sea salt

3 cups / 450g (2 15-oz. cans) chickpeas, drained and rinsed

1 Preheat the oven to 400°F / 200°C. In a small saucepan, melt the coconut oil over low heat. Whisk in the lemon juice, dill, onion powder, and salt. Remove from the heat, and cover to keep warm.

2 Spread the chickpeas out on a clean kitchen towel and rub them dry, discarding any loose skins (the chickpeas will not crisp in the oven if wet). Place the chickpeas in a large bowl and toss them with the coconut oil mixture.

3 Spread the chickpeas on a large rimmed baking sheet lined with parchment paper and roast, stirring occasionally, until golden and crisp, 25 to 35 minutes.

4 Remove the chickpeas from the oven. Let them cool and serve at room temperature. Store in an airtight glass container at room temperature for up to 1 week.

ROLLOVER Use these in place of the croutons in the Grilled Caesar Salad with Chickpea Croutons (page 61).

SPICY-SWEET PUMPKIN SEED SNACKS

At this point in the cookbook, you may be aware of how obsessed I am with salty-sweet combinations. The one-two punch of this flavor coupling strikes a primordial chord that tells our brains we're satisfied, so I try to include a touch of both in almost everything I make. These immensely fulfilling (and addictive) nibbles are the perfect thing to whip up as an alternative to crackers or cookies when I host friends for tea. The maple syrup gives the seeds a hint of sweetness and balances the salty tamari notes and the hit of spice. Try them at cocktail hour instead of fried and sodium-heavy prepared nuts, or snack on them instead of chips during a movie. They also are great sprinkled on top of soup or salad.

SERVES 4 ————————————————————

2 teaspoons coconut oil, melted

1 tablespoon pure maple syrup

1 tablespoon gluten-free tamari or soy sauce

¼ teaspoon ground cumin

¼ teaspoon red chile powder

⅛ teaspoon smoked hot paprika (ground chipotle would also work)

1 cup / 150g raw, unsalted pumpkin seeds

1 Preheat the oven to 300°F / 150°C. Line a rimmed baking sheet with parchment paper.

2 In large mixing bowl, whisk together the coconut oil, maple syrup, tamari, cumin, chile powder, and paprika. Add the pumpkin seeds and stir to coat. Pour the seeds onto the prepared baking sheet, spread them out evenly without too much overlap, and place in the oven.

3 After about 10 minutes, remove the seeds from the oven and stir them, again making sure they are evenly spread out. Roast for 7 to 10 minutes more, then stir the seeds and spread them out evenly again, this time ensuring that the seeds *are* touching but not piled on top of one another. Roast for 2 to 3 minutes more, then remove from the oven and let them cool for at least 15 minutes without disturbing them.

4 When the seeds are cool, lightly break them apart into small portions; they should stick together in free-form, lacy sections. If needed, transfer them to a paper towel to absorb any excess oil. Store in an airtight container at room temperature for up to 1 week.

ROLLOVER These are delicious crumbled on top of the Cashew Corn Chowder with Chipotle Oil (page 38).

SUNBUTTER RYE TOASTS

with Salted Maple Strawberries

3 cups / 400g raw, unsalted, shelled sunflower seeds

Cold-pressed olive oil (optional)

2 teaspoons ground cinnamon (optional)

½ teaspoon fine sea salt (optional)

4 slices whole-grain rye bread

1 batch Salted Maple Strawberries (recipe follows)

ROLLOVER Use the extra sunflower butter and make the Double Chocolate Chunk Sunbutter Cookies (page 228) or as a substitute for the almond butter in Brilliant Banana Almond Soft-Serve (page 221).

Living in Denmark has given me a deep appreciation for rye bread. It's not just popular here, it's an everyday staple that you'll see sitting on the counter like a glorious, malty brown brick, no matter whose home you're in. This recipe is a quick little snack that really satisfies. Homemade sunflower seed butter (or "sunbutter") is simple to make and a delicious alternative to peanut butter. Here I've paired it with toasted dark rye and strawberries that have been macerated in maple syrup and a little salt to bring out their sweetness. This combo is also delicious on top of yogurt or ice cream, morning oats, or even blended into a smoothie, if you have any leftovers.

SERVES 4 ————————————————————

1 Preheat the oven to 350°F / 180°C.

2 Place the sunflower seeds in an even layer on a rimmed baking sheet and toast until golden and fragrant, 10 to 15 minutes. Remove them from the oven and let cool.

3 Place the cooled sunflower seeds in a food processor and pulse, occasionally scraping down the sides, until smooth and creamy (this process can take 10 minutes or more, so be patient). If the seeds are not releasing their oil, add a little olive oil to help the process along. Once the mixture is creamy, add the cinnamon and sea salt, if using, and blend to incorporate. Store the sunbutter in an airtight glass jar in the fridge for up to 1 month.

4 To assemble, toast the rye bread until dark around the edges. Spread the desired amount of sunbutter over the toast and top with the Salted Maple Strawberries. Serve immediately.

SALTED MAPLE STRAWBERRIES

SERVES 2 TO 4

Hull and quarter the strawberries, and place them in a bowl with the maple syrup and salt. Crush a few berries with a fork on the side of the bowl and stir to mix the juices with the syrup. Let the strawberries marinate at room temperature for 5 to 10 minutes, then enjoy over toast.

(V) (GF) (R) (GrF)

Generous ½ pint / 250g strawberries

1 tablespoon pure maple syrup

Pinch of fine sea salt

SWEET POTATO DATE MUFFINS

DRY INGREDIENTS

1 cup / 150g whole-grain wheat flour

2 teaspoons baking powder

½ teaspoon baking soda

2 teaspoons ground cinnamon

1 teaspoon ground ginger

¼ teaspoon fine sea salt

1 cup / 100g rolled oats

1 cup / 150g chopped dates

WET INGREDIENTS

¼ cup / 60ml coconut oil, melted, plus more for greasing the muffun tin

2 ripe bananas

1 cup / 275g sweet potato purée (from about 1 large roasted sweet potato)

⅓ cup / 80ml pure maple syrup

2 teaspoons pure vanilla extract

¾ cup / 185ml plant-based milk of your choice

OPTIONAL ADD-INS

Handful of chopped raw, unsalted pecans

Zest of 1 orange

There is a vegan café in Toronto that serves *the best* muffins, but when a local reporter revealed the nutrition analysis, I—along with everyone who loves them—was completely shocked at how high the fat, salt, and calorie contents were. I set out to make a *much* more virtuous version with all the yumminess of the original. Sweet potato purée and banana bind the ingredients together (so you can skip the eggs), while adding a light, natural sweetness to the batter. Studded with juicy dates and rolled oats, these muffins are perfect as a snack when you're on the go or as a light breakfast. Add the optional orange zest and pecans for even more flavor and texture.

MAKES 12 MUFFINS

1 Preheat the oven to 375°C / 190°C. Lightly grease a 12-muffin tin with coconut oil and set it aside.

2 In a large bowl, sift together the flour, baking powder, baking soda, cinnamon, ginger, and salt. Add the oats and stir to combine.

3 In a food processor, pulse to combine the bananas, sweet potato purée, maple syrup, coconut oil, vanilla, and milk. Pour these wet ingredients over the dry ingredients and stir to combine, using as few strokes as possible. Fold in the chopped dates and optional add-ins.

4 Drop a few tablespoons of the batter into each muffin cup and bake until they are golden, fragrant, and pass the toothpick test, about 30 minutes. Store leftover muffins in an airtight container in the fridge for up to 5 days, or in the freezer for 1 month.

SPICY WATERMELON MOJITO ICE POPS

Inspired by the popular cocktail, I've taken the classic lime-and-mint combination to the next level. The coolness of the frozen watermelon and mint with a spicy wink of cayenne is surprising and delicious. If you are making these for kids, you can certainly reduce or omit the cayenne, but the adults in your life will undoubtedly appreciate the sophisticated kick in these beauties—like eating fire and ice at the same time!

MAKES 10 ICE POPS ———————————————————————

2¼ pounds / 1kg seedless watermelon flesh

¼ cup / 60ml freshly squeezed lime juice

2 pinches of cayenne, as desired

2 tablespoons pure maple syrup or raw honey, plus more for the molds

3 tablespoons fresh mint leaves, plus more for the molds

1 Cut the watermelon into chunks, remove the rind, and place the flesh in a blender. Blend on medium-low speed until the mixture is liquefied. Strain the juice through a sieve into a jug with a spout and press the pulp to extract as much juice as possible. Discard the pulp.

2 Return the juice to the blender and add the lime juice, cayenne, maple syrup, and mint leaves. Blend just enough to chop the mint—do not go too far or you'll change the color of the juice. Let the mixture steep for 10 minutes to infuse the juice with the mint. You should end up with at least 3 cups / 750ml of liquid.

3 Brush a little maple syrup on one side of the remaining mint leaves and press them to the insides of the ice pop molds—it helps to use a chopstick. Use 2 or 3 leaves per mold. (This is purely for aesthetics, so if you're pressed for time, skip this step.)

4 Carefully pour a portion of the watermelon juice mixture into each mold, insert the wooden sticks, and set the molds in the freezer for at least 3 hours. To remove the pops from the molds, run the molds under warm water for a few seconds until the pops release.

ROLLOVER The juice alone from this recipe is totally incredible. Leave out the cayenne and add a touch of sparkling water for a refreshing summer drink.

HONEY ALMOND
GRANOLA BARS

2 cups / 200g rolled oats

1 cup / 135g raw, unsalted
almonds (hazelnuts, pecans,
and walnuts are also
delicious here)

2 tablespoons coconut oil

½ cup / 125ml raw honey

½ cup / 125ml tahini

1 teaspoon pure vanilla
extract

½ cup / 85g unsulfured
dried fruit (raisins, dates,
figs, prunes, apricots, or
a combination), roughly
chopped

1½ cups / 55g puffed
whole-grain cereal (such as
rice puffs)

¼ teaspoon flaky sea salt

I grew up with a granola bar in my lunch bag every day, and no matter how old I get, I know I will always love biting into a sweet, gooey, nutty treat. These bars are the perfect on-the-go snack and hopefully will replace the store-bought varieties, which are often loaded with hidden processed sugars and fats.

It's important to toast the oats and almonds here, as both contain an unwanted compound called phytic acid, which is destroyed by heat. The bonus to this step is gaining heaps of extra flavor from toasting the nuts and grains. Feel free to change up the dried fruit: raisins, dates, prunes, cranberries, and figs are all tasty options.

MAKES 14 BARS

1 Preheat the oven to 325°F / 160°C. Line a brownie pan with plastic wrap or parchment paper.

2 Place the oats and almonds on a rimmed baking sheet, trying to keep them as separate as possible, and bake, stirring once or twice, until the oats are golden and have a toasted aroma, 12 to 15 minutes. Remove from the oven, let cool, and roughly chop the almonds.

3 In a small saucepan, melt the coconut oil over low heat. Add the honey, tahini, and vanilla; whisk until combined. Remove from heat.

4 In a large bowl, combine the oats and almonds with the dried fruit, puffed cereal, and salt. Pour the wet ingredients over the dry and stir quickly.

5 Spoon the mixture into the prepared brownie pan and, using slightly damp hands, press it firmly into the pan, especially around the edges and corners. Set the pan in the fridge for a couple of hours to firm up, then remove and slice into 14 bars. Store the bars in an airtight container in the fridge for up 2 weeks, or wrap them individually for to-go snacks.

BRILLIANT BANANA ALMOND SOFT-SERVE

If you've had people over for dinner in the last decade, you'll probably be familiar with the challenge of feeding someone with a food intolerance or a lifestyle that doesn't include dairy, eggs, gluten, sugar . . . *whatever*. Well, now you can definitely say that you have dessert covered, because this ice cream checks all the boxes, no matter what the restriction!

Frozen bananas miraculously whip up to make the creamiest, most delicious soft-serve ice cream on their own, but roasted almond butter, vanilla, and a little sea salt make this dessert really special. If you or someone you are serving has a nut allergy, feel free to use seed butter (such as sunbutter, page 212) instead of the almond butter, or omit it altogether.

2 ripe bananas

1 to 2 tablespoons almond butter (or your preferred nut/seed butter)

¼ teaspoon pure vanilla extract

Pinch of fine sea salt

SERVES 1 TO 2 ———————————————————————————

1 Peel the bananas and break them into small chunks. Place them in a sealed plastic bag in the freezer for at least 8 hours.

2 Remove the bananas from the freezer and let thaw just slightly, 5 to 10 minutes. In a food processor, combine the bananas, almond butter, vanilla, and salt. Purée until smooth and creamy. Serve immediately.

COCONUT CARDAMOM BLUEBERRY
SNACK CAKE

Coconut oil, for greasing the pan

DRY INGREDIENTS

1 cup / 90g unsweetened desiccated coconut, plus a little extra for garnish

1 cup / 100g rolled oats

1 cup / 170g whole-grain wheat flour

1½ teaspoons baking powder

½ teaspoon baking soda

1 to 2 teaspoons ground cardamom (depending on your preference)

¾ teaspoon fine sea salt

WET INGREDIENTS

1 14-oz. / 400ml can full-fat coconut milk

Zest of 1 lemon

2 tablespoons freshly squeezed lemon juice

2 teaspoons pure vanilla extract

¼ cup / 60ml pure maple syrup

2 large eggs

1 cup / 115g blueberries, fresh or thawed frozen

There are two kinds of people in this world: those who like frosting and those who do not. I fall into the latter camp and was one of those freaky kids who scraped the thick layer of sugar-schmear off her birthday cake and gave it to her best friend. Now that you know this about me, you'll understand my motivation for making this snack cake. Because there is no frosting, it is easily portable and handheld. I dialed down the sweetness that you would normally find in a dessert cake, so keep that in mind when you're enjoying it. The benefit of this is that you can definitely eat this cake for breakfast! Who can argue with that?

MAKES 16 PIECES ————————————————————————

1 Preheat the oven to 350°F / 180°C. Lightly grease an 8 × 8-inch / 20 × 20cm brownie pan with coconut oil.

2 In a large bowl, combine the dry ingredients: the coconut, oats, flour, baking powder, baking soda, cardamom, and salt.

3 In a medium bowl, whisk together the wet ingredients: the coconut milk, lemon zest and juice, vanilla, maple syrup, and eggs. Pour the wet ingredients over the dry ingredients and stir to combine in as few strokes as possible. Fold in the blueberries. Pour the batter into the prepared pan. Sprinkle with the remaining coconut.

4 Bake until a toothpick comes out clean when inserted into the middle of the cake, 35 to 40 minutes. Let the cake cool completely, then slice it into 16 squares. Store in an airtight container in the refrigerator for up to 5 days.

TOASTED WALNUT BROWNIE BITES, 3 WAYS

One of the most successful recipes on my blog is undoubtedly the Raw Brownie. With its super-short ingredient list, foolproof method, and wildly delicious results, it's no wonder that so many people have opened their mind to healthier sweets because of it. If you want to keep the base recipe as it is, be my guest! But I've given you three other options to suit a number of tastes. If you're making these for a buffet or party, for instance, it's fun to offer a few variations.

Store the brownies in the freezer until you're ready to serve them. Although delicious at room temperature, they are also really good cold.

BROWNIE DOUGH

MAKES 1 POUND / 500G OF DOUGH —————————————

1½ cups / 130g raw, unsalted walnuts

¾ cup / 70g cocoa powder

¼ teaspoon fine sea salt

2 cups / 300g soft dates (preferably Medjool)

1 Preheat the oven to 350°F / 180°C.

2 Place the walnuts on a rimmed baking sheet and toast until they are lightly colored and fragrant, 7 to 10 minutes. Remove from the oven and let them cool.

3 In a food processor, pulse the walnuts until they are finely ground. Add the cocoa and salt. Pulse to combine.

4 Pit the dates and add them one at a time through the feed tube of the food processor while it is running. You should end up with a mixture that resembles cake crumbs but, when pressed, will easily stick together (if the mixture does not hold together well, add more dates).

5 Use the dough to make the Brownie Bites that follow. Leftover dough will keep in the freezer for up to 1 month.

ESPRESSO BROWNIE BITES

MAKES ABOUT 10 BALLS

Combine the dough with the espresso powder, using your hands to fully incorporate the ingredients. Shape the dough into 10 small bite-size balls. Freeze the balls until ready to eat. Store in the freezer for up to 1 month.

⅓ batch (about ⅓ pound / 165g) of Brownie Dough (page 224)

¾ teaspoon espresso powder

VANILLA COCONUT BROWNIE BITES

MAKES ABOUT 10 BALLS

Combine the dough with the vanilla and 1½ teaspoons of the coconut, using your hands to fully incorporate the ingredients. Shape the dough into 10 small bite-size balls, then roll them in the remaining coconut. Freeze the balls until ready to eat. Store in the freezer for up to 1 month.

⅓ batch (about ⅓ pound / 165g) of Brownie Dough (page 224)

1 teaspoon pure vanilla extract

3 tablespoons unsweetened desiccated coconut, toasted

SPICED ORANGE BROWNIE BITES

MAKES ABOUT 10 BALLS

Combine the dough with the orange zest, cinnamon, and cayenne, if desired, using your hands to fully incorporate the ingredients. Shape the dough into 10 small bite-size balls. Freeze the balls until ready to eat. Store in the freezer for up to 1 month.

⅓ batch (about ⅓ pound / 165g) of Brownie Dough (page 224)

Zest of 1 orange

¼ teaspoon ground cinnamon

Pinch of cayenne (optional)

DOUBLE CHOCOLATE CHUNK
SUNBUTTER COOKIES

2 large eggs

2 teaspoons pure vanilla extract

1 cup / 250g / 250ml sunbutter (page 212)

½ cup / 125ml pure maple syrup

1 teaspoon baking soda

¼ teaspoon fine sea salt

½ cup / 45g cocoa powder

3½ ounces / 100g dark chocolate (70% or higher), roughly chopped

1¼ cups / 170g raw, unsalted, shelled sunflower seeds

I'm pretty convinced that whatever your question might be, these cookies are the answer. They are miraculously made without a speck of flour, instead using sunflower seed butter as their base, which yields a super rich, moist, and satisfying result. They are surprisingly cakey and unapologetically fudgey with their dark chocolate chunks (not chips—a crucial distinction). The sunflower seed coating around the outside adds a wicked crunch and textural balance to the chewiness, but you could use another type of seed or nut if you like—chopped hazelnuts would be divine.

MAKES 20 COOKIES

1 Preheat the oven to 325°F / 160°C. Line a rimmed baking sheet with parchment paper.

2 In a small bowl, whisk together the eggs and vanilla. Add the sunbutter and mix thoroughly. Add the maple syrup, baking soda, and salt and fold together. Sift in the cocoa powder and stir to incorporate. Fold in the chopped chocolate.

3 Place the sunflower seeds in a separate bowl. Wet your hands slightly with water. Divide the dough into about 20 portions and roll each into a rough ball (the dough will be very wet, but this is normal!).

4 Drop the dough balls into the bowl of seeds and roll to coat them in the seeds. Flatten the balls out slightly and place them on the prepared baking sheet about 2 inches / 5cm apart.

5 Bake the cookies for 10 to 13 minutes, until they have risen and expanded. Let them cool slightly before serving. Store the cookies in an airtight container at room temperature for up to 1 week.

BUYING AND STORING KITCHEN STAPLES

The following ingredients are what I would consider kitchen staples, and for that reason it's important to invest in good-quality versions of them. If you can't get some of these things at your local store, I think they are worth a trip to the health food store (or order them online), since you will be using them very frequently.

Cold-Pressed Olive Oil

Buying: When purchasing olive oil, look for a product in a dark glass bottle. Light destroys the delicate nutrients in the oil, so it's essential that the colored glass is green, brown, or blue, not clear. Never purchase olive oil in a plastic container. It's okay to purchase oil sold in a tin, but be sure to transfer it to a dark glass bottle when you get home. Look for the terms *unrefined* and *cold-pressed* on the label, meaning that it was extracted on the first pressing, processed at lower temperatures without chemicals, and still contains the most nutrition and flavor.

Storing: Olive oil will keep for 2 to 3 months after opening, so buy only the amount you need and use it up before then. Store it away from heat: in the refrigerator or in a very small bottle in a relatively cool, dark place.

Coconut Oil

Burned and oxidized fats cause free-radical damage in the body (that means no more cooking with olive oil!), so it's important to cook with oils that have a high smoke point. Coconut oil is a great choice.

Buying: To avoid coconut's overwhelming flavor, choose expeller-pressed, steam-refined, non-hydrogenated coconut oil, which has a neutral taste. Cold-pressed virgin coconut oil has a strong flavor and is best with raw foods.

Storing: Because it is so stable, coconut oil can be stored at room temperature for up to 1 year. If coconut oil comes packaged in plastic, transfer it to a glass jar.

Soy Sauce and Tamari

Soy sauce comes in two varieties: light and dark. The light one is lighter in color with a low viscosity and is extremely salty. This type is more expensive than the dark and is used as a condiment at the table. Dark soy sauce is deep in color with a higher viscosity and a sweeter flavor (usually due to additives such as caramel color or molasses). Dark soy sauce is used more frequently in cooking. Tamari is my top pick for soy-based sauces, because it is gluten-free (check the label—it must say gluten- and wheat-free). Tamari is traditionally brewed, has a stronger flavor than soy sauce, and is best used to season longer-cooking foods, such as soups, stews, and baked dishes.

Buying: I highly recommend purchasing good-quality soy products whenever possible. Look for the terms *traditionally brewed*, *organic*, and *non-GMO*. The conventional and less expensive versions of this seasoning may contain food dyes, refined sweeteners, preservatives, and chemical residues from processing.

Storing: Opened soy condiments will keep in the fridge for 2 to 3 months.

Fine and Flaky Salt

There are two types of salt I use on a daily basis: fine and flaky sea salt. Fine sea salt is good for seasoning during cooking and, of course, baking, because it is easy to measure and dissolves evenly. Flaky sea salt, sometimes called finishing salt, has a coarse texture that makes it easy to pinch between your fingers and sprinkle onto cooked foods as a garnish or to adjust the seasoning. Avoid table salt—it is highly refined with many additives and has an unpleasant, bitter aftertaste that can spoil the delicate flavors of food (plus, after processing, table salt can be just as harmful as processed white sugar—although it is generally eaten in much smaller quantities).

Buying: When purchasing salt, look for all-natural, dried (not boiled), unrefined salts with no added ingredients. Sea salt and Himalayan crystal salt are the types I use most often.

Storing: Store salt in glass, ceramic, stone, or wood containers (do not store it in metal, or it will corrode the container), or keep small amounts in a salt cellar on your counter for easy access. Salt will keep indefinitely if stored in a dry, clean environment.

Black Pepper

Black pepper does not have to be expensive, but I do insist that it is ground fresh in a pepper mill.

Buying: Always purchase whole black peppercorns. For my recipes, I like a medium-coarse grind from a pepper mill. Invest in a good mill, grind your own, and your life will be forever changed.

Storing: Store whole black peppercorns as you would all spices, in an airtight container away from heat and light. Peppercorns will keep for 1 to 2 years.

Lemon

When a recipe in this book calls for lemon juice, I am referring to freshly squeezed lemon juice from the real citrus fruit, not the liquid in a yellow plastic lemon (which contains preservatives and sulfites).

Buying: I call for lemon zest quite often in this book—it has a ton of flavor! For this reason, try to buy organic lemons if you can find them. But if you can only find conventional lemons, wash them really well.

Storing: Lemons kept in an airtight bag in the refrigerator will stay juicy and fresh for up to 1 month.

Apple Cider Vinegar

Apple cider vinegar adds delicious zing to all kinds of foods and is perfect for pickling. It is rich in enzymes, aids digestion, alkalinizes the body, and supports a healthy immune system—truly a miracle food!

Buying: Made from fermented apple cider, apple cider vinegar should always be purchased

SHOPPING REMINDERS

The grocery store can be an overwhelming place, especially if you are trying to make healthier choices. Keep these tips in mind on your next trip to the store.

Stick to the outside. The perimeter of every grocery store is where you'll find the freshest things: fruits, vegetables, bread, eggs, and dairy, with produce typically situated right near the front door. This is where you'll want to spend the bulk of your time (and budget). Lastly, take a quick trip to the center aisles to grab dried staples such as grains, beans, and spices. If your store has bulk bins, use them! Buying dried goods in bulk, instead of in packages, is often far less expensive.

Read labels. In general, only purchase things with one ingredient ("chickpeas," or "almonds," for example). If you are buying packaged items, watch for terms that are vague and misleading: *all natural*, *fresh*, *healthy*, *whole-grain*, *diet*, *lite*, *no added sugar*, *fortified*, *enriched*, *low-fat*, and *fat-free*. Even packaged food labeled as organic should be scrutinized, because such a label refers to the agricultural process, not the food's health properties. Just because the food is organic doesn't necessarily mean it's good for you—white sugar can be made organically too!

Make a list. Writing down and sticking to a shopping list will help save you time, money, and energy in the store. Try to keep your impulse buys to the produce aisle.

unpasteurized (raw), unfiltered with "the mother" (the cobweb-like strands of good bacteria in the vinegar), and organic, if possible. Look for it in glass bottles.

Storing: Apple cider vinegar is highly acidic, so it can last for many months outside of the refrigerator without spoiling, but keeping it in a cool, dry place away from direct sunlight, such as in a pantry cupboard, is still important. If you know that you won't be using it very often, I suggest keeping it in the fridge.

Pure Maple Syrup

Maple syrup is by far my favorite sweetener, conveniently gluten-free, vegan, and easy to find.

It's true that it may be more expensive than other sweeteners, but I believe it is worth the investment for both taste and nutrition.

Buying: When purchasing maple syrup, it's essential to read the ingredients list—it should have only 100 percent pure maple syrup listed. Avoid buying a product that contains maple flavor, high-fructose corn syrup, or other sweeteners, or that is labeled with the terms *pancake syrup* or *breakfast syrup*. If your grocery store offers different grades of maple syrup, choose Grade B over Grade A. Grade B maple syrup is from sap that is collected later in the season, is deeper in color, far more flavorful, and contains higher amounts of minerals.

Storing: Open bottles of pure maple syrup should be stored in the refrigerator and will keep for up to 1 year.

Herbs

Fresh herbs are not just a garnish in my recipes; they are a critical element that can take a weeknight meal to great heights and help transform a humble pot of brown rice into something special. Most people's main complaint about herbs is that they buy a bunch for a teaspoon or so to use in one recipe and the rest of it rots in the fridge! I hope the recipes and Rollover ideas in this book give you plenty of ideas and reasons to use every last scrap of your fresh herbs.

Buying: Purchase fresh herbs that look perky and vibrant, without any signs of discoloration, bruising, mold, or slime.

Storing: It's *essential* that you wash your herbs as soon as you get them home from the store, as dirt, debris, and bacteria will cause them to decay more rapidly. I fill my salad spinner with just enough water to cover the herb. Holding the stems, I dunk the herbs up and down into the water several times—as the dirt and debris run off, the water may change color. If the water is very murky, I repeat until it is clear, then drain the bowl and gently spin the herbs dry.

For tender herbs like cilantro, dill, mint, and flat-leaf parsley, cut off the ends as you would with flowers, place them in a glass with about 1 inch / 2.5cm of water in the bottom, and cover them with a plastic bag, sealing it as tightly as possible at the bottom with a rubber band. Stored this way, tender herbs should keep for 2 to 3 weeks in the refrigerator. The only

exception is basil, which should be stored at room temperature without a bag over top.

Wrap washed, sturdy herbs like rosemary, thyme, and sage in a paper towel and place them in a resealable plastic bag in the fridge. Sturdy herbs should keep for 2 to 3 weeks this way.

Flour

There aren't many recipes in this book that use flour, but the ones that do call for 100 percent whole-grain, whole wheat flour. If your supermarket sells other whole-grain flours, such as spelt, I always recommend using that over whole wheat.

Buying: The biggest indicator of a good-quality flour is that it has an expiration date listed on the package. Remember: Real food goes bad! Look for *100 percent whole-grain* flour from a grain such as wheat.

Storing: Because flour actually expires and turns rancid, it is extremely important to store whole-grain flour in an airtight canister in a cool, dry place. Store it in the freezer if you use it only occasionally.

Bread

Having a loaf of quality bread stashed in your freezer can be a lifesaver when you need to make a satisfying meal or snack in a pinch. Keep one or two varieties on hand, like a dark rye and/or a grainy country-style loaf.

Buying: Fresh is best! The first ingredient in high-quality bread should be 100 percent whole-grain, whole wheat (or other grain). I always recommend a sourdough loaf instead of one leavened with yeast, because it's far easier to digest and stays fresher about three times as long. Bonus points for finding a bread with sprouted grains, legumes, nuts, or seeds in it!

Storing: Bread will keep in an airtight bag at room temperature for about 3 days (any longer and you can bet it has preservatives in it). I like to slice my bread and store it in the freezer. This way, I can take out as many slices as I need at a time and let them thaw at room temperature or put them directly into the toaster. Frozen bread will keep for 6 months if tightly wrapped and sealed. Bread will get stale far faster in the refrigerator than at room temperature, so avoid storing it in the fridge.

ACKNOWLEDGMENTS

My name may be the one on the cover, but there are so many people whose energies and spirits played a major role in bringing this book to life.

First, to my husband, Mikkel, for taking the journey with me again. I feel so lucky that we have had the opportunity to truly collaborate on this, because your brilliant ideas, your ability to make sense of my nonsense, and your puns make everything so much better. I love you almost as much as tahini. Really close.

To my little star, Finn, for taste testing your way through the book with me and giving me very clear feedback. I hope you're not turned off chiles, lemons, or raw garlic for the rest of your life. My heart bursts when you beg for more lentils and the fact that you could identify almost every single piece of produce at the grocery store before you could say your own name makes Mama so proud.

To my family, Sheila, Paul, Diana, Trevor, and Ali, for agreeing to surf this wave with me once again. Thank you for your patience, encouragement, and belief in my dreams. I feel as if I can hear you cheering across the ocean every time I nail another recipe and take another photo that captures how delicious it is. And a special thanks to my mom for grocery shopping, chopping, cooking, and cleaning right alongside me. I love you all so much.

To the incredibly generous hands and souls who lovingly donated their precious days to help me in the kitchen: Signe Ågård Christensen, Mia Signe Kähler Albek, Mere Rosenbluth, and Gertrud Sol. Your energy was outrageous, contagious, and made each day more fun than it should have been. I love that your enthusiasm matched mine so we could celebrate the true joys of sharing food. What a gift you all are.

To Samantha, who has constantly supported and believed in me for so many years now. Look what we have done together! Thank you for creating a space for me to share my passions with the world and for always being on my side.

To my editors, Rica Allannic and Angelin Borsics, for constantly pushing me to think bigger, better, and beyond. Your patience, open-mindedness, and meticulousness really make this book shine. And to the rest of the Clarkson Potter team for all of your hard work, including Terry Deal, Heather Williamson, La Tricia Watford, Natasha Martin, and Stephanie Davis.

To Sharon Bowers, who took the mystery and pressure out of this whole process. You always find a way to make me see the big picture and give me permission to be a human who doesn't always know the answer. Your guidance, support, and professionalism mean the world to me.

To Rune Lundø, for once again bringing the best out of my images. I have so much fun learning from you, and I bow to your genius.

To Per Bo, for inspiring me with your beautiful ceramic works and for loaning many of the pieces shown in the book. You are a true artist and friend.

To my incredible recipe testers, who worked so hard and shared your thoughtful feedback with me. Your sincerity and critical assessments helped shape the recipes to be the best they can be. I am eternally grateful to you all: Bettina Abaou, Neeza Adenan, Amal Alhaag, Liz Ball, Renee Barker, Sheila Britton, Stephanie Bonic, Laura Chimelski, Kathryn Coatsworth, Signy Coatsworth, Michelle Cossar, Michele Delios, Anastasia Doudakis, Jenneke Dubois, Kelly Ekardt, Rickard Engstrom, Paula Hannon, Jules Hau, Brigitte Hendrix, Ngoc Hoang, Sharman Howes, Barbara Jacops, Gina Johnston, Kaitlin Kazmierowski, Renee Kemps, Alicia Key, Julie Leach, Debbie Levy, Kristine Lye, Jane Matthews, Shane Mazandarani, Kelly McCabe, Lisa Muller, Adrienne Murphy, Steph Nambiar, Jennifer Northrup, Valerie Orviss, Kinga Pulcinska, Mere Rosenbluth, Natasha Staddon, Ambar Surastri, Jaime Tan, Myra Tay, Misla Tesfamariam, Linda van der Heijden, Alison and Lexie Von Hahn, Aga Wala, and Ali Wylie.

And to all of the My New Roots readers, your love humbles me to no end. Your willingness to embrace new things and strive toward a healthier life has helped shape and define my purpose in this life. Without you, this cookbook would not exist, and I would get up in the morning to make breakfast just for myself, instead of the hundreds of thousands of you who care to see what I put on top of my smoothie bowl. I am so grateful to be a part of this community.

INDEX